Contents

Introduction

Why should you spend your valuable time learning to program in PROLOG?

It is fairly well accepted in the rapidly changing world of micro-computing that some significant developments will occur during the next ten years or so. Firstly there will be dramatic changes in hardware: higher processing speeds, greater on-board and back-up memory capacities, all at much reduced costs.

Secondly the software or programs which we use to drive the hardware will also be transformed, and as this is the means by which we communicate with the hardware, these changes will be more significant for us as users. It is reported that the Japanese have chosen PROLOG as the language which they are developing for their 5th Generation machines which are expected to be ready by the mid-1990s. This fact alone has generated considerable interest in the language, in both academic and business circles. Experts are claiming that the language of the 1990s will be PROLOG or a compromise language using the best features of PROLOG and another language such as LISP. Other experts claim that a multi-lingual approach is best—to use that language which is best suited to solving a particular problem.

So part of the answer to why you should learn to program in PROLOG is to make an investment in the future—to learn the rudiments of the language will give you a real insight into how languages are developing, and into the directions which software will take in the next few years.

Another part to the answer is less easy to specify clearly, but it goes like this. If nothing else the computer ought to be able to help us with our intellectual and knowledge-based activities, to help us thread our way through the myriad of facts and figures which surround us in our everyday lives. To a certain extent in the business world this is already happening in a limited way. It has barely started to happen in education and in our everyday activities. This is mainly because the languages which have so far been available have not been at all suitable for knowledge-based intellectual activities. PROLOG is suitable. Even in its infancy it lets you get the feel of how a program can be written to set up a knowledge-base, and how that base can be used to look for new perspectives on that knowledge.

This all sounds rather grand, but what do I mean by the term **knowledge-base**? The term is used to mean not only a quantity of data, but also the rules which relate to this data. By **data** I mean 'facts and figures'. If I were collecting data about wild birds I might very well have at my finger tips data about the dimensions, weight and number of sightings of certain birds in a given period of time. This data would be numeric, having been derived from measurements made by experts over many years. I may also have data about colourings, nesting habits and habitats. This data would be textual and descriptive. Your knowledge-base would also include rules by which you determine the various types of birds; e.g. the aquatic from the tree- and ground-dwelling types. The rules would extend to allow you to distinguish the various families of birds: to tell divers from ducks, gulls from auks, game birds from pigeons and doves, and so on.

So a knowledge-base is a collection of facts and figures together with a set of rules which relates to this data. Now in traditional programming languages, FORTRAN, BASIC, Pascal and the like, the storing of the data, the facts and figures, is relatively straight-forward requiring a small degree of technical know-how, but the process of establishing a set of rules is very tedious, and technically quite difficult. This is because the languages were not designed for this type of exercise. On the other hand PROLOG was designed just for this sort of activity.

Another significant difference between PROLOG and other more popular languages is the way in which the data is stored in the machine. PROLOG is designed to be a data-base and query language, and so the ease with which data is entered must be one of its main features. You will find that you commence programming in PROLOG by entering data right from the start, in the form of simple sentences. 'Brutus murdered Caesar' can be thought of as nouns representing two facts, Brutus and Caesar, bound together in a simple sentence by the relating verb 'murdered'. Entering data in the form of simple sentences resembles more closely the way in which we handle data processing in everyday life, making PROLOG a more 'natural' language to use.

The name PROLOG stands for PROgramming in LOGic. The language was devised in 1972 at the University of Marseilles, with the main purpose of assisting with the task of proving mathematical theorems, hence its firm base in formal logic. Since then and until quite recently, the language has only occasionally been implemented, and then only on main-frame or mini-computers mainly in the USA. It has come out of the closet in the last year or so when the Japanese recognised its data-base and query potential as the basis for their knowledge-based systems projected for the 1990s.

There are a dozen or so versions of the language now available. The revival of interest in the UK has been very strong and mainly centred on a research and teaching teams at Imperial College, London. The dialects of the language used at Imperial College have been designed and marketed by the software firm Logic Programming Associates (LPA), who have implemented the language on several microcomputers, including the IBM PC and compatibles, Research Machines 380Z and Nimbus, and BBC Model B and Master, Sinclair Spectrum, and most recently and probably the most significant for the future, the Amstrad range of Personal Computers. This LPA version of PROLOG is called micro-PROLOG, because it has been specifically written for micro-computers. It has been written with the beginner in mind as well as the professional, and includes in its facilities a special introductory version of the language called SIMPLE.

I use the SIMPLE version of micro-PROLOG throughout the book, and most of the examples are written in this dialect. In Chapter 10 I show you how easy it is to re-write the programs in the book in the Standard form of micro-PROLOG. Thus the book will give a thorough introduction to the language and prepare you for that particular dialect of the language which will emerge as dominant over the next year or so. Currently it is assumed that it will be very similar if not identical to the Standard version of Chapter 10. SIMPLE does, however, give us a slightly more friendly introduction initially. In the package marketed by LPA for the IBM PC and compatibles and RM Nimbus all of the dialects are available including the Edinburgh syntax.

If you have done some programming before you may have looked through the book in search of flowcharts, or some other method of describing how PROLOG programs work. You will have found none. When using PROLOG the inner workings of the machine and the language are almost completely hidden from

A PROLOG Primer

Clive Prigmore

Principal, Orpington College of Further Education

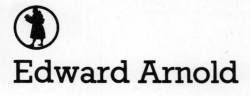

Edward Arnold

First published in Great Britain 1987 by
Edward Arnold (Publishers) Ltd, 41 Bedford Square, London WC1B 3DQ

Edward Arnold (Australia) Pty Ltd, 80 Waverley Road, Caulfield East,
Victoria 3145, Australia

Edward Arnold, 3 East Read Street, Baltimore, Maryland 21202, USA

British Library Cataloguing in Publication Data

Prigmore, Clive
  A PROLOG Primer.
  1. Prolog (Computer program language)
  I. Title
  005.13′3   QA76.73.P7

ISBN 0-7131-3640-5

Text set in 10 on 11 point Univers Linoterm
by Keyset Composition, Colchester, Essex
Printed and bound by J. W. Arrowsmith Ltd, Bristol

your view. Only very occasionally do we need to ask ourselves how a program works. To a very large extent PROLOG lets you get on with the programming, without having to bother about how the machine is going about its processing.

This book is aimed at the average reader, neither too academic nor one looking simply to be amused. I have aimed at explaining the rudiments of the language as simply and as directly as possible. In this brief span I have not exhausted the techniques of PROLOG nor entered into complicated explanations of its syntax, but hope to have given a good enough grounding in the basic principles to allow you to work on with it independently. I am sufficiently confident of PROLOG's future to expect this and books of similar level to be followed in due course with many others, which not only develop the language further, but also give examples of actual working knowledge-bases for general use in both business and education.

I feel that PROLOG is a language which makes us take a closer look at what we mean by 'knowledge', and even the term 'intelligence'—the ability to seek and find new relationships in a body of given data. You will see that the word **relationship** is the key to PROLOG. To this end right from the start I have tried to include examples from a wide range of disciplines, Biology, Geography, Statistics, etc. to name but a few, to give you the feeling of the breadth of possibilities which the language opens up. I have tried to avoid the trivial 'Peter and Jane' types of examples: 'Jane likes Peter', 'Peter likes the-dog' and so on, choosing as far as possible meaningful examples.

I have tried to get through the fundamental ideas as quickly as possible. The crux of the language is in learning to write **rules**, and this point is reached by the end of Chapter 2. I have left your path as uncluttered as possible with the technicalities of the language. The more technical points I have collected together and reserved until Chapter 3. Chapter 4 is all about how you do arithmetic in micro-PROLOG, but until you reach that point there is not a number in sight. Several examples are worked through in each chapter, and you are left with a handful of exercises to try on your own. The answers to these are either given at the end of the book, in which case they are marked with a *, or developed as examples later in the text. I have not left you with long lists of exercises to do, for this is designed to be a self-instruction book not a text-book for classroom use.

By about Chapters 7 and 8 you have been introduced to the main programming techniques, and I spend time looking at problem solving and developing larger programs. The problems which arise here are not amenable to quick simple solutions, and so in some cases answers are not given. But you will find that there are many worked Examples in the text which can be treated like Exercises if you wish, by attempting to solve the particular questions before they are worked in the text. For the same reason it is here that the Summaries given earlier at the end of chapters stop.

Several books on micro-PROLOG have already been published. I have referred to those which I found most valuable in Chapter 10. How is *A PROLOG Primer* different from these? Firstly I feel that most of the earlier books on micro-PROLOG have been written by academics for academics. Sometimes some of the problems considered have seemed rather esoteric, requiring considerable mental agility to follow the text in detail. This book aims to introduce the language to the complete beginner, or to someone who has done a little programming in another language such as BASIC. The techniques which I introduce are done carefully and thoroughly with ample Exercises and Examples, so that the reader can be sure at each stage that he/she has grasped the material.

I hope the text is readable in its own right, so that even if you did not have a machine with a micro-PROLOG interpreter at your disposal, you could derive considerable insight into the nature of the language. Obviously you will get most benefit from the book if you follow the text and work through the examples and exercises on a computer as they occur.

There is nothing left to do but to start work. If you have an IBM PC or compatible then at the operating system's **A**> all you have to do is to insert the micro-PROLOG disk and summon SIMPLE by continuing with something like **A**> **PROLOG LOAD "SIMPLE"** or even just **A**>**SIMPLE**. If you've got an Acornsoft version of micro-PROLOG for a BBC machine, then after you've switched on ***PROLOG** will give you access to the micro-PROLOG interpreter from ROM, and when you get the **&.** prompt you have to say **LOAD SIMPLE** to call up the SIMPLE module from disk, and when that is done you are ready to go. Good hunting with micro-PROLOG!

1
Setting up a data-base

1.1 Words and sentences

The main activity of PROLOG programming is to establish a data-base of facts. A glance at the ROYAL1 file on page 3 will give you an impression of what is meant by a data-base in PROLOG. It consists of a series of facts about the current Royal Family, and I have referred to the whole collection of facts as a file which I have named ROYAL1.

The first fact in this file is:

Elizabeth mother-of Charles

You should see this fact as two **objects** Elizabeth and Charles, bound together by the relationship **mother-of**, having the general form:

object   relationship   object

I shall refer to such statements of fact as **sentences**, and to their component parts as **words**. So in this case there are three words to the sentence. My early education is slightly offended by the term sentence because it does not contain a verb. It could just as well have been stored in the data-base as the sentence:

Elizabeth is-the-mother-of Charles

To keep the data input as simple and short as possible the **is-the** part of the sentence has been omitted, but is to be understood when read.

Please note that the relationship part of the sentence, whether **is-the-mother-of** or just **mother-of** is hyphenated, to join it together to make it one word or element of the sentence. So the first sentence of data is seen as having three words: **Elizabeth**, **mother-of**, and **Charles**.

1.2 Commands and characters

How do you get the data into the machine in the first place? Like all other programming languages micro-PROLOG gives you a set of commands for manipulating data and programs—e.g. for getting data into the memory of the machine from the keyboard, for outputting it to the screen or printer, for manipulating it when it is in memory, and for saving it on either tape or disk so that it can be loaded back into the machine for later use, and so on. The command for entering a sentence from the keyboard is **add**.

So, let's take up the story from the Introduction where you saw that to start a new session you call up PROLOG and LOAD SIMPLE, and the micro-PROLOG banner appears on the screen leaving you with the prompt:

&.

on the left-hand side of the screen. You would then continue by entering the characters **add(E** . . . one by one across the screen, until the whole line looks like:

&add(Elizabeth mother-of-Charles) [Return or Enter]

In the Acornsoft version of the language the cursor flashes under the **.** of the prompt, before you start entering a line. However, when the first character is entered, the **a** of **add** in this case, it over-writes the **.** leaving the line as shown above. I have shown the line ending with [Return or Enter] just to remind you that you have to hit the Return or Enter key at the end of every line to signal that as far as you are concerned the statement is complete and correct, and you want it to be stored in the machine's memory. If it is not correct the machine will soon tell you so, by means of one of its error messages—for details of these refer to your micro-PROLOG manual. So we have just entered our first program statement in micro-PROLOG.

This statement shows the main features of the structure of a statement in this language. The line starts with a command which operates on a data sentence which is enclosed in round brackets. Most versions of micro-PROLOG use lower case characters. Certainly the Acornsoft version would give you an error message if you tried to start the line with the command **ADD**, rather than **add**. The statement is divided up into its words and commands by using either spaces or brackets (or) as appropriate, and the whole statement is rounded off with the Return or Enter character.

These rules seem very simple indeed, but they have to be obeyed with great care. Particularly so when using the space—as I have already emphasised when describing the relation **mother-of**, without the hyphen it would have been read by the interpreter as two words, thus generating an error message. Extra spaces before and after the brackets (or) do not seem to upset the Acornsoft version, but I will not show spaces at these points and will try to keep a standard layout.

1.3   Syntax

You would expect a programming language which is based on logic to be fairly formal, so it is worthwhile at this early stage summarising more formally some of the above ideas.

The sentence form which I have introduced so far, of

object   relationship   object

and will depict by the cryptic <sentence>, is one example of what is usually referred to as the sentence **syntax**. You will meet different forms of sentence syntax in the course of the book. I will try to summarise them simply as they occur, for the sections on syntax in micro-PROLOG manuals often seem to be pretty heavy reading. The statement syntax as I have called it may thus be summarised as

command(object relationship object)

which can be depicted as command(<sentence>).

The grouping of the characters used in the words and sentences themselves is often referred to as the **lexical** syntax. The rule here is fairly simple: keyboard characters grouped into words obeying the sentence syntax given above, with words separated by spaces or brackets, and statements separated into lines by the Return or Enter symbol.

1.4   The **accept** and **list all** commands

After that brief digression into the 'nuts and bolts' of the language, I will carry on with the task of entering the data-base shown in the ROYAL1 file. We have entered only the first sentence so far, but the next three could be entered in a similar way:

> **&add(Elizabeth mother-of Anne)**
> **&add(Diana mother-of William)**
> **&add(Diana mother-of Henry)**

This is fine for four sentences, but what if there were 40 or 400? The command **add** and the relationship **mother-of** are repeated in all of the input lines. We can cut out the need to keep repeating these by using the **accept** command, and thus reduce the labour of inputting data somewhat. The **accept** command signals to the system that we want it to accept a relationship, so we proceed

> **&accept father-of**

and the machine responds with the prompt

> **father-of.**

with the cursor hovering under the **.** as before, and we continue completing the lines thus:

> **father-of(Philip Charles)**
> **father-of(Philip Anne)**
> **father-of(Charles William)**
> **father-of(Charles Henry)**
> **father-ofend**
> **&.**

The prompt **father-of.** will keep appearing on the left side of the screen until the word **end** is entered, at which point you are returned to the micro-PROLOG general **&.** prompt. The objects for the relationship **father-of** are entered as pairs of words in brackets.

The effect of entering these pairs of objects or words for the **father-of** relationship is the same as entering the four individual sentences using the **add** command for the **mother-of** relationship. You can convince yourself of this reasonably well by issuing the **list all** command. Its effect is shown in the ROYAL1 file.

> **&list all**
> **Elizabeth mother-of Charles**
> **Elizabeth mother-of Anne**
> **Diana mother-of William**
> **Diana mother-of Henry**
> **Philip father-of Charles**
> **Philip father-of Anne**
> **Charles father-of William**
> **Charles father-of Henry**
> **&.**

The ROYAL1 file

1.5   Binary and unary relationships

I started by considering relationships between two objects, usually called **binary** relationships, because it is easy to explain and grasp a relationship between two things. There is a simpler relationship in micro-PROLOG, and that is the **unary** relationship. In normal terms this would be interpreted as just a single feature or characteristic of the object. In this instance I wish to add into the data-base the characteristic that Elizabeth, Anne and Diana are female, and the rest male. For the unary relationship the micro-PROLOG sentence has the form:

object   relationship

e.g.   **Elizabeth is-female**

but as before, for simplicity I will miss out the verb **is-**, and proceed as below:

      &add(Elizabeth female)
      &add(Anne female)
      &add(Diana female)

I could have used the **accept** command, as I will now for entering the males:

      &accept male
      male(Philip)
      male(Charles)
      male(William)
      male(Henry)
      maleend
      &.

1.6   The **list** (relationship) command

If you now continue the line after the **&.** prompt, so that when completed it looks like

      &list female

you will get

      Elizabeth female
      Anne female
      Diana female
      &.

and

      &list male
      Philip male
      Charles male
      William male
      Henry male
      &.

The complete data-base, ROYAL2, is shown below.

> **&list all**
> **Elizabeth mother-of Charles**
> **Elizabeth mother-of Anne**
> **Diana mother-of William**
> **Diana mother-of Henry**
> **Philip father-of Charles**
> **Philip father-of Anne**
> **Charles father-of William**
> **Charles father-of Henry**
> **Elizabeth female**
> **Anne female**
> **Diana female**
> **Philip male**
> **Charles male**
> **William male**
> **Henry male**
> **&.**

The ROYAL2 file

The effect of the **list** (relationship) command is to show that the sentences which have been input are stored in groups according to relationships: all of the facts relating to **mother-of** are stored together, as are all those for **father-of**, **female** and **male**. In fact, if you had entered the sentences in no particular order jumbling them up for different relationships, you would find that when you said **list all** the sentences would have been grouped and output to the screen according to their relationships. They would be grouped for their particular relationship into the order in which they were entered into the machine. We will return to the use of this property of the language in greater detail later in the book.

EXERCISE 1.1

Compose a data-base of the facts given in Table 1.1.

Table 1.1

Cities	Countries	Relationships
Lyon	France	city-in
Paris	UK	member-of
Birmingham	Italy	capital-city
London	Netherlands	
Milan	Norway	
Rome	Sweden	
The-Hague		
Oslo		
Bergen		
Stockholm		

Organise the facts in the following way:

> city city-in country
> country member-of EEC
> city capital-city

EXERCISE 1.2*

Compose a data-base of the facts given in Table 1.2.

Table 1.2

Animals	Attributes	Relationship
birds	legs	animals-with
frogs	scales	
crocodiles	fur	
lizards		
snakes		
fish		
tigers		
humans		
horses		
dolphins		
whales		

For those non-biologists among us, you have to realise that not only humans but also dolphins and whales are classed as having fur.

1.7   Some simple 'nuts and bolts'

Micro-PROLOG does give you some very useful line editing features, and it is tempting to digress at this early stage to describe them in detail for your use; but I think that to do so would distract you from the general exposition of the language itself. On the other hand you do not wish to start entering even modest amounts of data without being able to make essential corrections when they are needed.

The data sentences which we have considered so far have been quite short, and it would be no great imposition to re-enter a sentence. So I suggest for a start that if there is an error in a particular sentence you delete the whole sentence and just re-write it correctly. The sentences are stored in blocks for a particular relationship in the order in which they were entered. For example, if you look at the ROYAL2 file you will see that **Philip father-of Anne** is the second fact in the block **father-of**. Let's pretend that you had spelt **Anne** as **Ann** and wished to correct it. You could proceed:

> &delete father-of 2
> &add 2 (Philip father-of Anne)

If you had listed the data-base in between the **delete** and the **add** you would have seen that the original sentence had been deleted. If instead of saying **add** 2(. . . you had just said **add** (. . . then the corrected sentence would just have been added to the foot of the **father-of** block.

You do not wish to enter even a modest data-base without being able to save it, so that you can use it in the future without having to re-enter it. Micro-PROLOG uses the familiar **load** and **save** commands, in the form:

> **load**<filename>   and   **save**<filename>

In the Acornsoft version these commands become

SAVE":1.$.ROYAL2"** and **SAVE":1.$.CITIES" and **SAVE":1.$.ANIMALS"**

for the three files which I have considered so far, with similar statements for loading: **LOAD":1.$.ROYAL2"** and so on.

I will go into more detail about the nuts and bolts of the language in Chapter 3.

1.8   Asking questions with the **is** command

The whole point of creating a data-base is to collect together and store safely a body of related facts which can be referred to when necessary. It is usually assumed that the amount of data to be stored is greater than is convenient to carry in one's head, and that speed of access to the data is another important factor which makes storing it on paper inappropriate. The act of referring to, or asking questions of, or querying the data-base is usually given the grand name **interrogation**.

A simple act of questioning is to look for facts which are hidden away in the depths of the data-base, and this is the type of activity which I will describe in this first chapter. But, a more important and interesting type of interrogation is when you search for new relationships which exist between facts in the base. One of micro-PROLOG's greatest strengths is the ease with which it allows us to look for new relationships within a body of data. I will start here by looking at some simple interrogation activities.

The first very simple activity is to ask whether a sentence is in the data-base at all. To do this you use the **is** command. I still have the ROYAL2 file in the workspace of the machine, and start at the **&.** prompt with:

> **&is(Elizabeth mother-of Anne)**
> **YES**
> **&.**

The syntax of the **is** command then is

> **is**(sentence)

or

> **is**(object relationship object)   for binary facts

or

> **is**(object relationship)   for unary facts

The response to the question 'Is Elizabeth the mother of Anne?' is seen to be 'Yes' as you would expect. The answer to the query 'Is Philip the mother of Anne?' is also equally predictable:

> **&is(Philip mother-of Anne)**
> **NO**
> **&.**

Slightly less predictable is the response to the query:

> **&is(philip father-of Anne)**
> **NO**
> **&.**

If you are used to using a computer you will not be surprised by the fact that it sees the word **philip** as being different from the word **Philip**. The pattern of characters which makes up the words in the sentence in the question must be identical to the pattern of characters in the data-base, for the answer to the question to be 'Yes'. The 'Yes' is then technically seen as a confirmation of the question 'Is it true that the following pattern of characters is in the data-base?' A 'No' means that it is not true, or that it is false.

1.9   Questions using variables with the **which** command

In itself the **is** question is not particularly interesting at first glance. It just gives confirmation that a particular sentence exists in the work-space, but does not tell you anything about it. The **which** command is much more explicit.

You want to be able to ask the data-base 'Which sentences have the following form: — **father-of Henry**'. It is really just a sentence completion test. Write in the word or words which complete the following sentences:

> — **mother-of Anne**
> — **father-of Henry**
> **Charles father-of** —

and so on.

Instead of entering — for the word in the data which we are looking for, micro-PROLOG uses a **variable** symbol. When there was an unknown factor in a maths problem at school, you would be taught something like 'Let's call the unknown quantity **x**'. We do a similar sort of thing in micro-PROLOG. We use the symbol **x** to stand for something which is as yet unknown, but for which we expect to find a value in due course. In fact it may have more than one value as the base is searched for the pattern match. So, as its value may vary, such an entity is called a variable. Using **x** to represent a variable the above sentence completion phrases look like:

> **x mother-of Anne**
> **x father-of Anne**
> **Charles father-of x**

The **which** command in use looks like:

> **&which(x:x father-of Henry)**
> **Charles**
> **No (more) answers**
> **&.**

It says 'Which word is found such that it completes the sentence — **father-of Henry**?' In this particular example it does not require any stretch of the imagination to personalise the question to mean 'Who is the father of Henry?', but we are concerned more with how PROLOG works for the moment.

Now we ask 'Which word or words are found in the data-base such that they complete the sentence **Charles father-of**?' Or, if you like the more particular approach 'Who is Charles the father of?'. Remembering distant English lessons you will realise that the **x** acts like a pronoun:

> **&which(x:Charles father-of x)**
> **William**
> **Henry**
> **No (more) answers**
> **&.**

The syntax of the **which** command is

which(variables: <sentence>)

or 'Which answer pattern exists such that it matches the given sentence pattern?' **Sentence pattern** because variables are sometimes substituted for the actual data objects in the data-base. So in this case <sentence> is used to mean sentence pattern.

The **:** symbol is read as 'such that' as it is in set notation in mathematics, for those of you who have met sets. You should be careful with the spaces adjacent to the **:** and round the second **x**. The Acornsoft version of micro-PROLOG is fairly forgiving in a liberal use of spaces here, but not all versions of micro-PROLOG will be. Note also how the machine scans the data-base in its work-space and outputs the value of the variables which match the given pattern, and then tells you that it can find **No (more) answers** to your queries, and then returns you to the **&.** prompt.

As you can imagine much of the activity of micro-PROLOG programming is about the manipulation of variables, so there is much of this to come for your delight. For the moment I will stretch the ideas just a little bit further, by allowing us the luxury of two variables **x** and **y**,

    &which(x:x father-of y)

asks for the word at the beginning of the sentence with the relationship **father-of**, irrespective of the value of the second word.

    &which(x:x father-of y)
    Philip
    Philip
    Charles
    Charles
    No (more) answers
    &.

It is obvious that the machine has scanned through its data-base and picked out the four sentences containing the relationship **father-of** and output the value of **x** — the first word of the binary relationship — even though this meant repeating the same value of **x** twice over.

The next question asks for the second word of the same relationship:

    &which(y:x father-of y)
    Charles
    Anne
    William
    Henry
    No (more) answers
    &.

This gives us the children of the **father-of** relationship. If we use both variables in the question we get:

    &which(x y:x father-of y)
    Philip Charles
    Philip Anne
    Charles William
    Charles Henry
    No (more) answers
    &.

Ask silly questions and, thankfully, you will get sensible answers:

> **&which(x:x father-of x)**
> **No (more) answers**
> **&.**

This asks for the pattern which matches one word to itself. This is quite possible in general terms, but not if the data-base is to be consistent with the personalised idea of **father-of**, for no-one is his own father!

You can also use the idea of variables with the **is** command:

> **&is(x mother-of Henry)**
> **YES**
> **&.**

This asks the personalised question 'Is the mother of Henry known?' Or, 'Is there a word which matches the rest of the sentence **mother-of Henry**?'

1.10   Relationships

This seems a suitable place to consider more closely the use of the word **relationship**. I have been rather free with its use so far, at one point talking about pattern matching and the next about personalised relationships 'mother of' and 'father of'. In truth the word can mean both of these things, indeed whatever we want it to mean! In the case of the data in the ROYAL2 file it is easy to grasp what is meant by the term, and from our own personal experiences of family relationships we could easily generalise these sentences to give us further relationships, e.g. **son-of**, **daughter-of**, **uncle-of**, **aunt-of**, **brother-of** and so on, because these ideas have real and immediate meaning for us.

However, as I have emphasised several times, you must remember that the interpreter in the machine is really just matching patterns of characters, and that if the relationships mean anything other than this to us it is really due to the concepts which we as humans form. During the course of the book we will consider many different examples of data-bases. The idea of relationships between the various facts of these systems will be more abstract than the personalised ones which I have chosen to start the book with.

EXERCISE 1.3*

Using the CITIES data-base which you created as an answer to Exercise 1.1, as shown on page 16, form **which**-statements to ask the following questions.

(a)   Is Lyon a city in France, is Oslo a city in Sweden, and is Manchester a city in the UK?
(b)   Is Stockholm a capital city, and is Milan a capital city?
(c)   Is Sweden a member of the EEC, and is France a member of the EEC?
(d)   Which cities are in Italy?
(e)   Which country is Oslo in?
(f)   Which countries are members of the EEC?
(g)   Which organisation is UK a member of, which is Norway a member of?

EXERCISE 1.4*

Using the ANIMALS data-base which you formed as an answer to Exercise 1.2, as shown in the Answers, form **which**-statements to ask the following questions.

(a)   Do dolphins have fur, and do birds have fur?
(b)   Which features do crocodiles have, and which do horses have?
(c)   Which animals have fur, and which have legs?

Summary

1   Sentences
(a)   A fact is entered into a micro-PROLOG data-base as a sentence. We have met two types of sentence:

	Sentence form
Binary	object relationship object
Unary	object relationship

If I wish to talk about a sentence of any form in general terms I shall refer to it as <sentence>.

(b)   A statement has the form: command(<sentence>)
e.g.   **add**(<sentence>)
or   **add**(object relationship object) for a binary sentence.

add lets you add a sentence to your data-base.

(c)   **accept** lets you add several sentences with the same relationship to the data-base. It has the form:

accept relationship
relationship(object object)
relationship(object object)
. . . etc. . .   for a binary sentence.
relationshipend

2   Listing
(a)   **list all** lists all of the sentences currently in the computer's work-space.

(b)   **list** 'relationship' lists all of the sentences currently in the work-space for a particular relationship.

3   Queries
(a)   **is**(<sentence>) asks if a sentence is in the current data-base.

(b)   **which**(variables:<sentence>) displays those objects from a particular sentence pattern in the data-base which are represented by the variable symbols **x**, **y** or **z**.

I now use the term <sentence> to mean a general sentence pattern and not just a specific fact:

e.g.   specific sentence   **Philip father-of Anne**
       sentence pattern   **x father-of y**

So you can think of a sentence pattern as one which has some or all of its objects replaced by the variable symbols **x**, **y** or **z**.

2
Logic and rules

2.1 Introduction

My aim in this chapter is to show you how to ask more detailed questions of the data-base using the two logical operators **and** and **not**. When you have seen these operators in use in several examples you will readily follow how they can be used to write some simple rules which can be stored in the data-base along with the other sentences. These rules can be used to define new relationships for use in the data-base. This ability to define new relationships by making combinations of the original ones in the data-base is one of the great strengths of micro-PROLOG.

   It will be obvious to you that the rules which you create will depend very much on the relationships which you chose to start with in your data-base. In the ROYAL2 data-base we could have chosen to include relationships like **son-of** and **daughter-of** or **grand-father-of** right from the start; but starting with the ROYAL2 file as shown on page 5 we can create these new relationships by combining **mother-of** or **father-of** and **is-male** or **is-female**, and **father-of** twice, or **father-of** followed by **mother-of** to get **grandfather-of**. So, as with all data-bases, the rules and procedures associated with it depend on how you set up the data in it in the first place.

2.2 The **and** operator

To ask questions of the data-base as if the persons were real rather than just patterns of characters, you could ask: 'Is there someone in the file who is male and who has Philip as his father?'. This humanises the rather abstract pattern matching process which we have to imagine is happening inside the machine's memory. From the machine's point of view the question is more like: 'Is there an object associated with the relationship **male** which is also related to the object **Philip** by the relationship **father-of**?'.

   The statement which gets at this **father-of** and **male** relationship in micro-PROLOG looks like:

    &is(Philip father-of x and x male)
    YES
    &.

Having been assured that this relationship does exist in the data-base, you will then want to know who the **x** is, and

> **&which(x:Philip father-of x and x male)**
> **Charles**
> **No (more) answers**
> **&.**

tells you this.

By introducing a second variable into the query we can ask the more general question: 'Is there anyone in the data-base who is male and has a father? — note 'a father' this time is not just restricted to Philip as father. To find facts in the data-base with these more general relationships you could pose the question:

> **&which(x:y father-of x and x male)**
> **Charles**
> **William**
> **Henry**
> **No (more) answers**
> **&.**

And if you wanted the father and son data output you could change this query slightly to:

> **&which(y x:y father-of x and x male)**
> **Philip Charles**
> **Charles William**
> **Charles Henry**
> **No (more) answers**
> **&.**

You will now readily see how to identify a grandfather relationship, by applying the **father-of** relationship twice. To be specific, in the first place:

> **&which(x:x father-of Charles and Charles father-of William)**
> **Philip**
> **No (more) answers**
> **&.**

And to ask the same question in slightly more general terms:

> **&which(x:x father-of y and y father-of z)**
> **Philip**
> **Philip**
> **No (more) answers**
> **&.**

This tells us that Philip is a grandfather twice over in our data-base, and a more detailed question can show up the three generation link using three variables:

> **&which(x y z:x father-of y and y father-of z)**
> **Philip Charles William**
> **Philip Charles Henry**
> **No (more) answers**
> **&.**

The way that the **and** operator is used then is simply to join together two (or more) simple sentences in the data-base in which the facts are either stated explicitly, or represented more generally by the variable symbols **x**, **y** or **z**. The logical effect of the **and** function is to put greater constraints on the data output from the base, because both of the conditions in the two original sentences have to apply simultaneously. In the father-son relationship which we created above, the **x father-of y** and **y male** relationships had to apply simultaneously for output to occur.

We can summarise the interrogation procedure using the **and** operator in the following way:

is(<sentence> **and** <sentence>)

which(variables:<sentence> **and** <sentence>)

Obviously the use of <sentence> twice in the brackets implies that they are different sentences. To be more specific we could say: **is**(<sentence1> **and** <sentence2>), but this distinction is not really necessary, and is not usually made when summarising the syntax in this way.

2.3   The **not** operator

This operator is used in front of a simple sentence like **and** but the effect of **not** is to negate the sense of the sentence which follows it. If you wished to ask of the ROYAL2 file whether Elizabeth was mother to someone who was not male, you could enter the query:

&**is(Elizabeth mother-of x and not x male)**
YES
&.

If you wished to know which fact in the data-base this **combined** condition applied to then you would proceed:

&**which(x:Elizabeth mother-of x and not x male)**
Anne
No (more) answers
&.

And then in even more general terms if you wished to pick out all of the mother–child relationships where the child is not male, you could use the two variables **x** and **y** in the statement:

&**which(x y:x mother-of y and not y male)**
Elizabeth Anne
No (more) answers
&.

This is not very convincing because there is only the one combined relationship in the data-base, so let's ask for the **not female** relationship instead:

&**which(x y:x mother-of y and not y female)**
Elizabeth Charles
Diana William
Diana Henry
No (more) answers
&.

If you wished to pick out all of the mothers except Elizabeth you would have to proceed:

&which(x y:x mother-of y and not Elizabeth mother-of y)
Diana William
Diana Henry
No (more) answers
&.

You will have noted how I have used the **not** in conjunction with the **and** operator, specifying a variable (or variables) in the first simple sentence followed by the negated sentence. A statement of the form **&which(x:not x mother-of y)** would be all too ambiguous to have any useful meaning at all, for it would include all of the other binary relationships in the data-base. So, if asked, such a question is met with the **No (more) answers** rebuff.

The syntax of queries using **not** can be summarised in the following way:

is(<sentence> **and not** <sentence>)

which(variables:<sentence> **and not** <sentence>)

EXAMPLE 2.1

The CITIES data-base is my answer to Exercise 1.1 in Chapter 1.

.list all
Lyon city-in France
Paris city-in France
Birmingham city-in UK
London city-in UK
Milan city-in Italy
Rome city-in Italy
The-Hague city-in Netherlands
Oslo city-in Norway
Bergen city-in Norway
Stockholm city-in Sweden
France member-of EEC
UK member-of EEC
Italy member-of EEC
Netherlands member-of EEC
Paris capital-city
London capital-city
Rome capital-city
Amsterdam capital-city
Oslo capital-city
Stockholm capital-city
&.

The CITIES data-base

Form **which**-statements to ask the following questions.

(a)   What is the capital city of France?
(b)   Output all of the capital cities in the data-base together with their appropriate countries.
(c)   Which cities in the UK are not the capital?

(d)   Which cities are not in EEC countries?
(e)   Which cities are not capitals and not in EEC countries?

(a)   **&which(x:x city-in France and x capital-city)**
      Paris
      No (more) answers
      &.

(b)   **&which(x y:x city-in y and x capital-city)**
      Paris France
      London UK
      Rome Italy
      Oslo Norway
      Stockholm Sweden
      No (more) answers
      &.

(c)   **&which(x:x city-in UK and not x capital-city)**
      Birmingham
      No (more) answers
      &.

(d)   **&which(x:x city-in y and not y member-of EEC)**
      Oslo
      Bergen
      Stockholm
      No (more) answers
      &.

(e)   **&which(x:x city-in y and not y member-of EEC and not x capital-city)**
      Bergen
      No (more) answers
      &.

With long queries as in the statement in this last question, especially if you are using a screen display of only 40 characters width, it makes for overall clarity and ease of understanding if the statement is split up in the following way:

      &which(x:x city-in y
      1and not y member-of EEC
      1and not x capital-city)
      Bergen
      No (more) answers
      &.

The **1** at the start of lines 2 and 3 indicates that at that point there is one bracket needed to complete the statement, because in the lines above the Return key had been struck before the right-hand bracket which completes the statement had been entered. The bracket at the end of line 3 does complete the statement.

EXERCISE 2.1*

Using the ANIMALS data-base which was created as an answer to Exercise 1.2 in Chapter 1, and is shown in the Answers, form **which**-statements to ask the following questions.

(a)   Which animals have both fur and legs?
(b)   Which animals have fur but do not have legs?
(c)   Which animals with legs have neither fur nor scales?
(d)   What characteristics are possessed by those animals which do not have legs?

2.4   What about an 'or' operator?

If you've studied logic before and/or used logic operators with another programming language, you may well be asking this question. Usually you are given three logic operators to play with, viz 'and', 'or' and 'not'. Thus if you wished to get at the idea of 'parent' then you would want to form a question combining the two relationships **mother-of** and **father-of**. You would say that **parent-of** would be given by either **mother-of** or **father-of**. To explore this further to get at the idea of 'parent of Charles', you may be tempted to try:

> **&which(x:x mother-of Charles or x father-of Charles)**
> **Syntax error: X father-of Charles or X mother-of Charles**
> **not a valid sentence form**
> **&.**

The truth is that there is no specific 'or' function in the SIMPLE version of micro-PROLOG, but we shall see later that there is an **either** . . . **or** . . . operator. You can get at the data that this operator would generate by asking both questions separately:

> **&which(x:x mother-of Charles)**
> **Elizabeth**
> **No (more) answers**
> **&which(x:x father-of Charles)**
> **Philip**
> **No (more) answers**
> **&.**

For those who are interested in the more abstract ideas of logic, you will appreciate that you can derive all of the logic relationships with just two of the operators: 'or' with 'not', or 'and' with 'not'.

2.5   Rules

If the relationship **parent-of** is needed for the data-base in addition to the relationships **mother-of** and **father-of** then it would be quite acceptable to add these sentences into it as specific items of data. You would load ROYAL2 into your machine and then continue:

> **&add(Elizabeth parent-of Charles)**
> **&add(Elizabeth parent-of Anne)**
> **&add(Philip parent-of Charles)**
>   . . . and so on.

This would not only be tedious but also unnecessary. As I said in the Introduction one of the most powerful features of PROLOG is the way it lets you make up rules, or form new relationships from ones you already have in your data-base. To give us the relationship **parent-of** in terms of relationships which are already in the data-base, we say

He is a parent if he is a father of . . .

or

She is a parent if she is a mother of . . .

To turn these statements into micro-PROLOG sentences we must replace the pronouns 'he' and 'she', and the '. . .' with variable symbols **x** and **y**. The sentences would be:

x parent-of y if x father-of y

or

x parent-of y if x mother-of y

Now assume that we are back loading ROYAL2 into the machine, without the specific **parent-of** sentences given above. We would then continue:

&add(x parent-of y if x father-of y)
&add(x parent-of y if x mother-of y)
&.

Then to test that this new relationship has had the desired effect we would ask the question:

&which(x y:x parent-of y)
Philip Charles
Philip Anne
Charles William
Charles Henry
Elizabeth Charles
Elizabeth Anne
Diana William
Diana Henry
No (more) answers
&.

This gives the correct parent/child data. It is instructive to compare what you get from the data-base when you say:

&list mother-of
Elizabeth mother-of Charles
Elizabeth mother-of Anne
Diana mother-of William
Diana mother-of Henry
&.

and when you say:

&list parent-of
X parent-of Y if
**   X father-of Y**
X parent-of Y if
**   X mother-of Y**
&.

So you see that **list father-of** and **list mother-of** will give a list of the actual sentences in the data-base, whereas **list parent-of** does not give the sentences but the rule by which it may in its turn be used to generate the data.

No, it is neither a hallucination nor a typographical error that the **x** and **y** have changed into capitals, i.e. **X** and **Y**, in the listing of **parent-of**; but it is a subtle point which I will talk about in more detail in the next chapter on the nuts and bolts of the language. It is not a detail which changes significantly the meaning of what we are doing.

You can take these ideas one stage further and make up new rules using old ones. To derive the relationship **grand-parent** you could start with the initial enquiry:

> **&which(x y:x parent-of z and z parent-of y)**
> **Philip William**
> **Philip Henry**
> **Elizabeth William**
> **Elizabeth Henry**
> **No (more) answers**
> **&.**

And then turn it into a rule and add it to the data-base:

> **&add(x grand-parent-of y if x parent-of z and z parent-of y)**
> **&.**

and then test it with:

> **&which(x y:x grand-parent-of y)**
> **Philip William**
> **Philip Henry**
> **Elizabeth William**
> **Elizabeth Henry**
> **&.**

and see that you get the same result.

If you now said **list all** you would see on the screen the ROYAL2 file which you had before, with the rules we have added tacked on at the end which we shall call ROYAL3.

> **&list all**
> **Elizabeth mother-of Charles**
> **Elizabeth moth . . .**
>
> **. . .**
> **William male**
> **Henry male**
> **X parent-of Y if**
> **   X father-of Y**
> **X parent-of y if**
> **   X mother-of Y**
> **X grand-parent-of Y if**
> **   X parent-of Z and**
> **   Z parent-of Y**
> **&.**

The ROYAL3 file

The syntax of this rule making process can be summarised as follows, if we agree that the rule is seen as being embodied in a <new sentence>:

<new sentence> **if** <sentence>

or

    \<new sentence\> **if** \<sentence\> and \<sentence\>

or

    \<new sentence\> **if** \<sentence\> and not \<sentence\>

EXERCISE 2.2*

Starting with the ROYAL3 file derive **which**-statements to find the following relationships: (a) **daughter-of**, (b) **brother-of**, (c) **paternal-grandfather-of** and (d) **maternal-grandfather-of**. Turn these relationships into rules which could be added to the data-base.

EXAMPLE 2.2

Start with the CITIES data-base and create rules for (a) **capital-city-of**, (b) **EEC-city** and (c) **EEC-capital-city-of**, and test them using **which**-statements.

(a)   The rule for **capital-city-of** is:
> **X capital-city-of Y if**
> > **X city-in Y and**
> > **X capital-city**

and the **which**-statement to test this rule is:

> **&which(x y:x capital-city-of y)**
> **Paris France**
> **London UK**
> **Rome Italy**
> **Oslo Norway**
> **Stockholm Sweden**
> **No (more) answers**
> **&.**

(b)   The rule for **EEC-city** is:

> **X EEC-city if**
> > **X city-in Y and**
> > **Y member-of EEC**

and the **which**-statement to test it is:

> **&which(x:x EEC-city)**
> **Lyon**
> **Paris**
> **Birmingham**
> **London**
> **Milan**
> **Rome**
> **The-Hague**
> **No (more) answers**
> **&.**

(c)   The rule for **EEC-capital-city-of** uses rule (a) **capital-city-of** and adds to it membership of the EEC, as follows:

> **X EEC-capital-city-of Y if**
> > **X capital-city-of Y and**
> > **Y member-of EEC**

and the **which**-statement to test this is:

> **&which(x y:x EEC-capital-city-of y)**
> **Paris France**
> **London UK**
> **Rome Italy**
> **No (more) answers**
> **&.**

EXERCISE 2.3*

Using the ANIMALS data-base create rules for:

(a)   animals with fur
(b)   animals without legs
(c)   animals with fur and without legs.

EXERCISE 2.4*

A murder investigation has reached the stage where there are six suspects, which, to save space and typing effort, I have just named A, B, C, D, E and F. There are three main factors which lead to their being suspected: having a motive, having access to and knowledge to use the murder weapon, and finally having the opportunity to have carried out the deed. The situation is summarised in Table 2.1.

Table 2.1

	motive-is	access-to-weapon	opportunity-level
A	jealousy	No	high
B	financial-gain	Yes	medium
C	grudge	Yes	medium
D		No	high
E	financial-gain	Yes	low
F	grudge	Yes	high

Create a data-base with sentences of the form which I have indicated using suspect B.

> B **motive-is** financial-gain
> B **access-to-weapon**
> B **opportunity-level** medium

(a)   Find the motivation of those suspects whose opportunity level is high.
(b)   Find those suspects and their opportunity level for whom the motive is financial gain.
(c)   Find those suspects whose opportunity level is high and who have access to the weapon.
(d)   Define a rule called **strong-suspect** for suspects whose opportunity level is either medium or high.

(e)   Define a rule **prime-suspect** for those strong suspects who also have access to the weapon.

Summary

1   The **and** operator joins two sentences in the following way:

<sentence> **and** <sentence>

This conjunction may be used in query statements as in

is(<sentence> **and** <sentence>)

and

which(variables:<sentence> **and** <sentence>)

such that an output to the query is given only in those circumstances when both sentences are true.

2   The **not** operator acts on the <sentence> which follows it turning all of its true states false and vice versa. It is used in the following way:

<sentence> **and not** <sentence>
is(<sentence> **and not** <sentence>)
which(variables:<sentence> **and not** <sentence>)

The last two query modes give positive outputs only when the first sentence is true and the second false.

3   Rules and the **if** operator

(a)   Rules can be formed in micro-PROLOG as a new sentence for the data-base, and have the form:

<new sentence> **if** <sentence>
<new sentence> **if** <sentence> **and** <sentence>
<new sentence> **if** <sentence> **and** not <sentence>

(b)   They are added to the data-base by means of the **add** operator:

add(<new sentence> **if** <sentence> **and** <sentence>)

and so on for the other two forms.

(c)   The rule or new sentence can be queried with **is** or **which** as could the old sentences in the data-base. In the data-base the rule is stored as a conditional sentence of the form:

<new sentence> **if**
    <sentence> **and**
    <sentence>

You now have two types of sentence in the data-base: a simple sentence and a conditional one.

3
Nuts and bolts

In the Introduction I said that my main object was to get you writing programs in micro-PROLOG as quickly as possible, to give you the flavour of the language. If you are a complete beginner to computing then you may feel that so far there is a lot of introductory matter which has not been explained, and that you have been rather 'thrown in at the deep end'. In the course of the first two chapters I have occasionally given details about the maintenance of the programs, about the editing or saving for example, when I thought that these would be of immediate help; but I did not give summaries of these facts at the end of the chapters, or attempt to present them as a cohesive body of facts.

In this chapter I attempt to present some of these details in a more organised manner. If you are not new to computing then you will find them very straightforward and will be able to pass through the material very quickly. If you are then I hope you find that the chapter puts the earlier programming activities into clearer perspective.

3.1   PROLOG and the computer system

When a computer is in action there is a continuous flow of electronic traffic round the system, from keyboard to central processor to screen, from processor to disk unit and so on. This traffic is controlled by a set of programs which are permanently in the system — this set of programs is called collectively the **operating system**. If the system includes a disk drive in the traffic flow then the whole operating system is usually referred to as a **disk operating system**, or cryptically DOS. For the earlier 8-bit generation of micros CP/M (Control Program/Microcomputers) became the standard DOS, and for the newer 16-bit generation, which is largely dominated by the IBM range of machines, MS-DOS (MicroSoft DOS) is the standard. micro-PROLOG is available for machines with both CP/M and MS-DOS operating systems.

On the BBC micro the DOS is stored on a special ROM (Read Only Memory) chip which is plugged into the processor, as is the micro-PROLOG interpreter, but the SIMPLE program is stored on disk. With CP/M and MS-DOS machines micro-PROLOG and SIMPLE are stored on disk. What do we mean by **micro-PROLOG interpreter**, and what is the function of the SIMPLE program?

You have seen that micro-PROLOG programs consist of sentences, and that programming statements are commands which operate on these sentences. Obviously the machine does not understand these sentences and statements in the form in which we enter them, and so there has to be a program which translates them into electronic codes within the machine's processor. micro-PROLOG is the program which translates the sentences into electronic codes.

Originally PROLOG was devised for professional programmers on mainframe computers, and in this form is a rather unfriendly language, as you will see when we look at micro-PROLOG in its Standard form in Chapter 10.

To make the language easier to use and so more accessible to micro users like you and me, the original micro-PROLOG has been wrapped up in a collection of other programs, often referred to as **modules**. One of these programs is called SIMPLE and its main job is to let us enter facts in the form of the sentences, like those used so far, which are in what is called the **infix** form:

Elizabeth mother-of Charles

In the **prefix** form of the original micro-PROLOG, this sentence would become:

mother-of(Elizabeth Charles)

I'm sure you will agree that the infix form makes the fact look more like a sentence, and easier to follow in the first instance

There are several other programs in this collection or suite of programs which makes up micro-PROLOG, one of which is SIMTRAC (SIMple TRACe) which we will use in Section 3.6 to trace the way a program operates. SIMPLE is the main entry program into micro-PROLOG, and so is often referred to as the **front-end** program. This is why we started off with *PROLOG and then followed with LOAD SIMPLE to load in this front-end program.

The two functions which we have met, which must be common to PROLOG and micro-PROLOG and involve the DOS of the particular system which we are using, are the saving and loading operations where programs are passed to and from the disk and the work space of the machine. The **work-space** is just the area of memory which we are currently using for our program. In Chapter 1 I said that for the Acornsoft version of micro-PROLOG the commands for these two functions were:

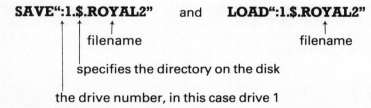

SAVE":1.$.ROYAL2"**   and   **LOAD":1.$.ROYAL2"

                    filename   filename

        specifies the directory on the disk

    the drive number, in this case drive 1

Note that for an MS-DOS machine with micro-PROLOG modules in the A-drive and programs in the B-drive this would become **LOAD"B:ROYAL2"**. The Acornsoft system in this case comprises a twin disk system with the drives numbered 0 and 1, shown as **:0** and **:1** in the file specification. The micro-PROLOG suite of programs is on drive 0, and the program files which I have created are on drive 1. The file names on each disk may be stored in separate directories. This assists with careful file naming, especially if you have a mixture of word processing, BASIC and micro-PROLOG files all stored on the same disk. Such a mixture is highly undesirable, of course, and you would be courting a disk disaster. However, if you store files in different directories on the disk, then you have to name the directories. In the above example $ is the name of the directory in which ROYAL2 has been stored.

The Acornsoft software is very forgiving in the matter of file specification. You could change all of the characters to lower case letters if you wished; and you could omit the $, the directory name, if you were sure that you were going to store on the disk only files of the same type, and that you were unlikely to make a mistake and use the same file name twice. So the two commands could look like:

save"**:l.royall**"   and   **load**"**:l.royall**"

The **.** is used to separate the two or three parts of the file specification.

3.2   Numbers and strings

In any programming language the two basic elements with which you work are **numbers** and **strings**. We are due to look at numbers in Chapter 4; but you will appreciate that numbers like 1987 or 3.142 or −273.2 are really just a group of digits (or number characters) entered one after the other at the keyboard. So you can think of a number as a string of digits, including possibly a decimal point (just the full-stop on the keyboard), and maybe a − or + sign as appropriate. If a string of such characters, beginning with a digit or − sign is entered into a program, then the interpreter (micro-PROLOG, BASIC or whatever) will try to interpret it as a number, i.e. an item of data which could be used in some sort of calculation, if it is in an appropriate place in the sentence. More of this in Chapter 4.

The words which we have used in data sentences must be seen as just strings of characters. The space is the main character which separates the words in a sentence. Brackets separate the sentence from the command which operates on it to turn it into a statement. Lines are separated from each other by pressing the Return key. So, we say that the syntactic separators are the spaces, brackets and the Return character. micro-PROLOG allows you to be generous with spaces where they are appropriate, i.e. between words, round variable symbols and round brackets. You must not include spaces within a 'word' though — e.g. if the English version of a relationship is 'is mother of' this must be entered hyphenated as 'is-mother-of'.

Deep inside the machine, however, characters are, of course, represented as numbers. All letters of the alphabet (upper and lower case are evaluated differently), punctuation marks and other symbols which appear on the keyboard of your computer have their own number code, called the ASCII code.

3.3   Editing

When you are entering characters at the keyboard they are not inserted into the work space until the Return key is pressed at the end of the line. Until then you can use the line editing features of the BBC micro with the Acornsoft version of micro-PROLOG. So, if you notice a mistake in the line, you can use the DELETE key to erase the characters entered up to that point, and re-write them. On an MS-DOS machine you would delete with the 'backspace' or ← key.

As I said in Chapter 1, you can re-write records in your data-base which you have found to be in error by deleting the offending sentence and then adding the corrected one. Remember that the facts are stored in blocks of relationships, so you can say:

delete(relationship number)

and follow this with:

add(number <sentence>)

where 'number' is the position of the sentence within the relationship block. If the position of the replacing sentence within the block is not important, then you could just say:

add(<sentence>)

and it would be added to the end of the particular relationship block. The effect of '**add**(number <sentence>)' is to insert the sentence into the position indicated by 'number', and of course the remainder of the sentences lower in that block have their numbers re-adjusted to take into account this insertion.

When the sentences are fairly short, and relatively dissimilar one from the other, then the 'delete-insert' method of editing just described is quite adequate and safe even though not very imaginative. However, the line editing facilities of the BBC micro do give more convenient editing features, and depend on the use of the Copy key. Let's look at some examples of the use of the Copy feature with **add**, **edit** and **cedit**.

The ROYAL2 file did not include the two sons Andrew and Edward of the current Royal Family. If we say **list mother-of** we get:

&list mother-of
Elizabeth mother-of Charles
Elizabeth mother-of Anne
Diana mother-of William
Diana mother-of Henry
&.

and then we continue:

&add 3 (. . .

Now, having entered the bracket as shown, you can move the cursor using the arrowed keys on the BBC keyboard up to the E for Elizabeth, and then press the Copy key until the end of **mother-of**, so that the last line on the screen will look like:

&add 3 (Elizabeth mother-of

You now have to enter **Andrew)** [Return] and the entry will be complete:

&add 3 (Elizabeth mother-of Andrew)

list mother-of will now give you a similar listing to that above, but the new sentence will appear at position 3.

If you had completed the above procedure but had made a typing error — your left little finger had hit q instead of w at the end of Andrew — you could continue

&edit mother-of 3

and

3 (Elizabeth mother-of Andreq)

will appear on the screen. If you now start by entering **3** on the left-hand side of the screen, and then move the cursor with arrow keys to the line above, you can use the Copy key to copy the line to include the e of Andreq on to your entry line, and then enter **w)** [Return]. The sentence will now be entered correctly.

This **edit** function has, however, over-written fact 3 of the **mother-of** block, which was what you wanted at the time. But you can use the **cedit** operator to edit and copy at the same time, **cedit** standing for 'copy-edit'.

&cedit mother-of 3

gives you

3 (Elizabeth mother-of Andrew)

on the screen.

If you now enter **4** on the left-hand side of the screen, and then move the cursor to the line above and Copy the line above as far as the end of **mother-of**, you can now enter **Edward** [Return], so that the whole of the line looks like

4 (Elizabeth mother-of Edward)

and after the Return this new record will be inserted into the 4th position of the **mother-of** block.

It takes much longer to describe than to do when you get into the habit of using the Copy facility regularly. It saves a lot of time when there are many very similar records to be entered into a file. Unfortunately there is no comparable copying facility on MS-DOS systems.

3.4   Printing and scrolling

Another very useful feature of the Acornsoft version of micro-PROLOG is the Print facility. If you hold down the control key, marked CTRL, and then strike the B key, and then release the CTRL key, this switches on the printer. From this point on everything you enter into the machine which appears on the screen will also appear on your printer when you press Return. To switch the printer off you have to repeat the procedure but now strike the C key while the CTRL key is depressed. This switching process is usually denoted CTRL/B and CTRL/C. In MS-DOS these become CTRL/P and CTRL/N.

Similarly if the file which you have entered is quite large then when you say **list all** it rolls up the screen, and maybe some of the sentences disappear off the top of the screen. You can stop this **scrolling** action of the screen so that you can look at parts of the file, by pressing CTRL/N, and start it again with CTRL/O. With an MS-DOS system you have to toggle the CTRL/S operation, that is first occurrence is ON, next is OFF and so on.

3.5   Miscellaneous operators and ideas

The rest of this chapter contains a miscellaneous collection of ideas. I will introduce the operators as they occur naturally in the solutions of the two chosen examples, rather than just list them. They are in general extensions to operators which we have met already, and give us additional facilities rather than completely new ones.

If you have been using a computer to enter programs you will already have made a few mistakes. The error messages which you receive on the screen in these instances play a vital part in your learning about the language. It is not feasible for me to contrive a set of typical errors and the resulting error message at this stage. Your only recourse really is to the manual of the system which you are using. Error message descriptions are not the strongest parts of any manual about any programming language — so good luck!

One thing which may have caused you some concern is the seemingly restricted range of variable names at your disposal in micro-PROLOG. So far I have used only three: **x**, **y** and **z**. You have seen how these are translated into **X**, **Y** and **Z** in the formation of rules. In fact there is a wide range of variable names which can be used simply by adding digits to the three variable names which we have used already. So, **x1**, **x2**, **x3**, **x4** etc., **y1**, **y2**, **y3**, **y4** etc., and **z1**, **z2**, **z3**, **z4** etc., are all valid variable names, as are the capital letter versions **X1**, **X2**, **X3**, **X4** etc. I will avoid using the capital letter versions in programs, so as to allow the change which occurs in rule formation to be more obvious. Just to ring the changes I will use variable names other than **x**, **y** and **z** in the following examples. Professional micro-PROLOG allow more meaningful variable names — refer to the Answer to Exercise 8.12.

EXAMPLE 3.1

The MURDER data-base with its rules is my answer to Exercise 2.4.

> **&list all**
> **A motive-is jealousy**
> **B motive-is financial-gain**
> **C motive-is grudge**
> **E motive-is financial-gain**
> **F motive-is grudge**
> **B access-to-weapon**
> **C access-to-weapon**
> **E access-to-weapon**
> **F access-to-weapon**
> **A opportunity-level high**
> **B opportunity-level medium**
> **C opportunity-level medium**
> **D opportunity-level high**
> **E opportunity-level low**
> **F opportunity-level high**
> **X strong-suspect if**
>   **X opportunity-level medium**
> **X strong-suspect if**
>   **X opportunity-level high**
> **X prime-suspect if**
>   **X strong-suspect and**
>   **X access-to-weapon**
> **&.**

The MURDER data-base

Sometimes it is convenient and possibly necessary to get a list of all of the relationships and rules in your data-base, without showing all of the other facts as well. The **list dict** command does this for you, as shown for the current Example (**dict** is of course short for 'dictionary').

> **&list dict**
> **motive-is dict**
> **access-to-weapon dict**
> **opportunity-level dict**
> **strong-suspect dict**
> **prime-suspect dict**
> **&.**

Sometimes instead of using the **which** command and getting all of the solutions to the query flashing down the screen, it is convenient to look at each solution in turn. The **one** command lets you do this. In this instance, instead of using the variable names **x** and **y**, I have rung the changes and used **x1** and **x2**. The query is the answer to question (a) in Exercise 2.4:

&one(x1 x2:x1 motive-is x2 and x1 opportunity-level high)
A jealousy
more?(y/n)y
F grudge
more?(y/n)y
No (more) answers
&.

You will notice that after each solution the system pauses and asks if you want more solutions — **more?(y/n)** appears on the screen and you have to answer **y** (yes) for the search for solutions to continue, or **n** (no) for it to stop.

A solution to question 2.4 (b) is given below still using the **one** command:

&one(y1 y2:y1 motive-is financial-gain
land y1 opportunity-level y2)
B medium
more?(y/n)y
E low
more?(y/n)y
No (more) answers
&.

The **all** command has the same effect as the **which** command as you can see from the program answer to question 2.4 (c):

&all(z1:z1 opportunity-level high and z1 access-to-weapon)
F
No (more) answers
&.

3.6   Tracing a solution

It is instructive to look at the way in which the micro-PROLOG system searches through its facts looking for the solutions to a particular query, especially when the query involves the conjunction of more than one fact in the data-base. Micro-PROLOG has a tracing module called 'simtrac' which is short for Simple Trace, which can be called up to trace each step in the evaluation of an expression, while searching for a solution.

If you have done some programming before you will have met the idea of **tracing** and be aware of both its strengths and weaknesses. Its strengths are obvious, that you can analyse each step along the route to a solution, which can help you understand a solution better, and find any defects in it should there be any. The weakness is that it usually fills your screen with so much detail about the solution that it is difficult to see the wood for the trees. These comments are just as pertinent in micro-PROLOG as in BASIC say.

To help you distinguish the wood from the trees, I have concocted a very simple example just for this tracing procedure.

EXAMPLE 3.2

Five people may be distinguished by the colour of hair and eyes, as shown in Table 3.1.

Table 3.1

People	Hair	Eyes
A	d	br
B	l	bl
C	d	bl
D	m	br
E	d	bl

For Hair the abbreviations are d:dark, l:light and m:medium.
For Eyes they are br:brown and bl:blue.

Yes, it is a very simple (simplistic) situation, and the coding is brief, but it is all in aid of keeping the words and sentences as brief as possible to allow you to follow the trace print-out. For this I composed a very simple data-base:

> **&list all**
> **A hair d**
> **B hair l**
> **C hair d**
> **D hair m**
> **E hair d**
> **A eyes br**
> **B eyes bl**
> **C eyes bl**
> **D eyes br**
> **E eyes bl**
> **&.**

The query which I am going to trace is to find all those people who have dark hair and blue eyes:

> **&which(x:x hair d and x eyes bl)**
> **C**
> **E**
> **No (more) answers**
> **&.**

To start the trace:

> **&load simtrac**
> **&all-trace(x:x hair d and x eyes bl)**

The way in which the conjunction of the two sentences is evaluated is to look for solutions of the first sentence first, and then when a solution to the first is found the system searches down the second sentence to find a solution for that too. When a solution to both conditions is found it is output. Then the system **backtracks** to where it left off in its second sentence search to look for another solution. And so on until all of the possible combinations have been tested.

   In the print-out of the trace shown in Trace Listing 3.1 the first sentence is labelled (1) and the second (2). There are 20 comparisons in this search. Five

&all-trace(x:x hair d and x eyes bl)

(1) : X hair d trace?y
matching (1) : X hair d with head of 1 : A hair d
    match succeeds: A hair d
(1) solved : A hair d
(2) : A eyes bl trace?y
matching (2) : A eyes bl with head of 1 : A eyes br
    match fails
matching (2) : A eyes bl with head of 2 : B eyes bl
    match fails
matching (2) : A eyes bl with head of 3 : C eyes bl
    match fails
matching (2) : A eyes bl with head of 4 : D eyes br
    match fails
matching (2) : A eyes bl with head of 5 : E eyes bl
    match fails
(2) failing : A eyes bl
retrying (1)

matching (1) : X hair d with head of 2 : B hair 1
    match fails
matching (1) : X hair d with head of 3 : C hair d
    match succeeds: C hair d
(1) solved : C hair d
(2) : C eyes bl trace?y
matching (2) : C eyes bl with head of 1 : A eyes br
    match fails
matching (2) : C eyes bl with head of 2 : B eyes bl
    match fails
matching (2) : C eyes bl with head of 3 : C eyes bl
    match succeeds: C eyes bl
(2) solved : C eyes bl
C

Annotations:

. . . found **A hair d**

the system now looks for possible match of **A eyes bl** with the 5 **eyes** facts

. . . this search fails

. . goes gack to **B hair 1**
. . . this search fails
. . goes on to **C hair d**
. . . this search succeeds

the system now looks for possible match for C eyes bl

. . . finds a match

. . . & outputs this solution

Trace Listing 3.1(a)

```
backtracking...

retrying (2)
matching (2) : C eyes bl with head of 4 : D eyes br
    match fails
matching (2) : C eyes bl with head of 5 : E eyes bl
    match fails
(2) failing : C eyes bl
retrying (1)

matching (1) : X hair d with head of 4 : D hair m
    match fails
matching (1) : X hair d with head of 5 : E hair d
    match succeeds: E hair d
(1) solved : E hair d
(2) : eyes bl trace?y
matching (2) : E eyes bl with head of 1 : A eyes br
    match fails
matching (2) : E eyes bl with head of 2 : B eyes bl
    match fails
matching (2) : E eyes bl with head of 3 : C eyes bl
    match fails
matching (2) : E eyes bl with head of 4 : D eyes br
    match fails
matching (2) : E eyes bl with head of 5 : E eyes bl
    match succeeds: E eyes bl
(2) solved : E eyes bl
E
backtracking...

retrying (2)

(2) failing : E eyes bl
retrying (1)

(1) failing : X hair d
No (more) answers
&.
```

the system **'backtracks'** to look at the remainder of the **eyes** facts

. . . this search fails

. . . goes back to **D hair m**
. . . and this search fails
. . . and on to **E hair d**
. . . this search succeeds

this system now looks for possible match for **E eyes bl**

. . . finds **E eyes bl**

. . . and outputs the solution

the system **'backtracks'** to look for more **E eyes bl** and retries **X hair d.**

Trace Listing 3.1(b)

comparisons of sentence (1) are needed to look for possible matches for **x hair d**. Three sentences satisfy this query: A, C and E. Each time micro-PROLOG finds such a match in sentence (1) it then moves on to search for matches for **x eyes bl** in sentence (2). So 15 comparisons are made in all for sentence (2), five for each of the three successful matches of sentence (1).

Please note again that when micro-PROLOG finds a match in sentence (2) and outputs the solution, it still goes back (**backtracks**) to the point in its search in (2) and completes its search through that list of sentences. It does not assume just because it has found a solution that there are no other solutions in the sentence (2).

What happens is shown in Trace Listings 3.1(a) and (b). I have annotated the print-out in an attempt to clarify what is happening and underlined the important points in the trace. Note that when it goes back to try a new sentence (1) it says **retrying (1)**, and when it goes back to continue its search through sentence (2) it says **backtracking** . . . .

The example is quite simple, but the resulting print-out is quite detailed. The traces of more complicated data-bases become quite horrendous. You will quickly get the impression that as far as the system is concerned, it is involved only in pattern 'matching', from the frequency with which it uses the term **match**. Even if it looks quite fierce, you will do well to study the print-out very carefully, until you are sure you understand exactly what it is doing. Better still, make up an example for yourself and try it on your machine.

Summary

As I said at the start of the chapter we have not broken new conceptual ground in this chapter, but have introduced a lot of practical ideas which should be useful to you in your programming activities. This is not a summary in the sense in which I have used and will use it in other chapters, but is more a check-list of terms and as such will help you to review the ground which we have covered.

operating system   disk operating system (DOS)   work-space
PROLOG SIMPLE   micro-PROLOG   interpreter   front-end
infix and prefix forms of sentences
save   load
filename   drive number   directory name
strings   numbers
sentences   statements
ASCII code

editing by means of **delete** and **add**
use of DELETE, COPY and arrowed keys
edit and cedit: edit relationship number

for the BBC range of micros
printer controls: CTRL/B printer ON, and CTRL/C for OFF
scrolling controls: CTRL/N for ON, and CTRL/O for OFF.

for MS-DOS systems
printer controls: CTRL/P printer ON, and CTRL/N for OFF
scrolling controls: CTRL/S as a toggle, first occurrence ON, next OFF, and so on.

more about variable names

list dict to list the relationships and rules in a data-base

    one(variables:\<sentence> **and not** \<sentence>)
    all(variable:\<sentence> **and not** \<sentence>)

load simtrac to load in the SIMPLE tracing module

    all-trace(variables:\<sentence> **and not** \<sentence>)

re-trying and **back-tracking**

4

Numbers

4.1 Introduction

In everyday transactions we use the term 'number' rather loosely: NPP 647L would pass as a car registration number, and ZH724658B as a National Insurance number. We would, however, use neither of these numbers to do any sort of calculation — they are used mainly for identification or coding purposes. In any programming language the term number is reserved for collections or strings of digits which may be used in some sort of calculation.

Micro-PROLOG was not really designed with 'number crunching' in mind, and so it does tend to handle numbers in a seemingly rather clumsy way. You will soon get used to its number foibles, and realise that it does make you think carefully about the fundamental arithmetic operations. For example, we are used in the normal state of affairs to the luxury of four arithmetic operators — add, subtract, multiply and divide — but in micro-PROLOG we are reduced to the bare essentials of add and multiply.

When using numbers in any programming language it is important to bear in mind that they come in various guises — whole numbers (integers) which are used for counting, decimal numbers which arise from measuring activities or from calculations — both of which may be positive or negative in nature. Further, computers have to make special provisions for very large numbers and very small numbers, i.e. numbers close to zero. With these factors in mind, let's have a look at how micro-PROLOG crunches its numbers.

4.2 Adding

We have used the command **add** to add facts to a data-base, so we must obviously look at a different word for the arithmetic function. This command is **SUM** — in capitals, because it is a standard micro-PROLOG command which is adopted without modification into SIMPLE PROLOG. In use **SUM** is a command which operates on three numbers in a bracket, which are separated by spaces, so this all looks like:

SUM(a b c)

The relationship between the numbers is that the third is always the sum of the previous two, or $c = a + b$, so we can express the statement as:

SUM(a b a+b)

However, you cannot use the statement on its own, but only in conjunction with either **is** or **which**. For example, with **is**:

>**&is(SUM(3 8 11))**
>**YES**
>**&.**

or

>**&is(SUM(17 7 34))**
>**NO**
>**&.**

This confirmation of whether a statement is true or not is not very interesting, but the use of a variable with the **which** command does extend the use of the **SUM** operator:

>**&which(x:SUM(4 13 x))**
>**17**
>**No (more) answers**
>**&.**

and

>**&which(x:SUM(3.973 46.82 x))**
>**50.793**
>**No (more) answers**
>**&.**

Some editorial advice is in order here. Don't forget the second right-hand bracket at the end of the statement! If you work in lower-case letters up to **SUM**, and then press the Caps or Shift Lock key, you may fall into the trap of entering **X** instead of **x**, later in the line. You will find the Copy function on the BBC micro invaluable here, because once you have got one statement on the screen, you can cursor up to it and copy **which(x:SUM(** . . . and just continue the expression in lower-case letters, thus not having to use the Shift or Caps Lock key at all after the first time. In fact many of the examples and exercises in this chapter can be entered by using the Copy function liberally, and just editing earlier statements on the screen.

I have so far used the variable **x** only in the third position of the triplet. What about expressions like:

>**&which(x:SUM(23.71 x 33.62))**
>**9.91**
>**No (more) answers**
>**&.**

What the statement is asking is 'What number must be added to 23.71 to give 33.62?', or you could read it as asking 'What number must be subtracted from 33.62 to give 23.71?', or more simply 'What number do you get if you subtract 23.71 from 33.62?'. The statement:

>**&which(x:SUM(x 19.24 12.43))**
>**−6.81**
>**No (more) answers**
>**&.**

asks the same sort of question 'What number do you get if you subtract 19.24 from

12.43?' In this case the answer is −6.81 a negative number, because 19.24 is greater than 12.43.

You can use only one variable in the statement.

    &which(x:SUM(x x 8.44))

will get you an error message for your trouble!

You will see that there are only three seemingly different ways in which the 'numbers' in the statement can be arranged:

    SUM(a b **x**)   **SUM**(a **x** b)   **SUM**(**x** a b)

where a and b stand for actual numbers, and **x** is the variable. In the first case **SUM**(a b **x**), **x** is the sum of a and b. In the second and third cases **SUM**(a **x** b) and **SUM**(**x** a b), **x** is the difference b−a, or b subtract a.

So you see that by arranging and reading the expressions in different ways we can make them perform additions or subtractions. The second and third expressions give the same results you will have realised, because a+x=b and x+a=b, or if you like a+x=x+a. Mathematicians would claim rather grandly that the expressions are commutative!

EXAMPLE 4.1

Write down the micro-PROLOG statements to find the values of the expressions below. The answers are given here immediately below the questions, so it will pay you to cover up the answers and treat these examples as exercises for you to do in the first place.

(a)   x=17.48+11.59   (b)   x=−7.52+3.71
(c)   x=4.83+(−3.72)   (d)   x=−1.98+(−5.63)
(e)   x=4.98−4.27   (f)   x=1.98−(−5.63)
(g)   x=9.18−(−11.82)   (h)   x=−23.62−(−14.91)

To save space I have given just the **which** statement, followed by the answer to the sum on the same line.

(a) **which(x:SUM(17.48 11.59 x))**   **29.07**
(b) **which(x:SUM(−7.52 3.71 x))**   **−3.81**
(c) **which(x:SUM(4.83 −3.72 x))**   **1.11**
(d) **which(x:SUM(−1.98 −5.63 x))**   **−7.61**
(e) **which(x:SUM(x 4.27 4.98))**   **0.71**
(f) **which(x:SUM(x −5.63 1.98))**   **7.61**
(g) **which(x:SUM(x −11.82 9.18))**   **21**
(h) **which(x:SUM(x −14.91 −23.62))** **−8.71**

I have used the **SUM** operator with whole and decimal numbers, both negative and positive. I have not so far looked at very large or very small numbers, but these considerations will arise more naturally when we look at multiplication and division.

4.3 Multiplying

The multiplication or product operator in micro-PROLOG is **TIMES**. It is used in the same syntactic way as **SUM** with the triplet of numbers as an **argument**. The expression has the form:

    TIMES(a b c)   where c=a*b

Computers use '*' rather than 'x' as the symbol for multiply, so that there is no confusion between 'x' for multiply and 'x' as a variable symbol. The expression can thus be stated as:

TIMES(a b a*b)

In words rather than symbols we can say: 'The third number of the triplet of numbers in the bracket is the product of the first two.' The statement is used with either the **is** or **which** operator as before with **SUM**. For example, with **is**:

    &is(TIMES(3 8 24))
    YES
    &.

or

    &is(TIMES(17 7 109))
    NO
    &.

Having seen how addition and subtraction were achieved in the number triplet of **SUM**, I expect that you have already guessed how multiply and divide will be obtained from the **TIMES** expression. So I will just give you a similar set of examples which you should in the first instance treat as exercises as before.

EXAMPLE 4.2

Write down the micro-PROLOG statements to find the values of the expressions below.

(a)   x=17.48*11.59   (b)   x=−7.52*3.71
(c)   x=4.83*(−3.72)   (d)   x=−1.98*(−5.63)
(e)   x=4.98/4.27   (f)   x=1.98/(−5.63)
(g)   x=9.18/(−11.82)   (h)   x=−23.62/(−14.91)

In this case I will give the full print-out for the eight questions — if you are not 100% certain of what is going on you should read it fairly carefully.

&which(x:TIMES(17.48 11.59 x))   (a)
202.5932
No (more) answers
&which(x:TIMES(−7.52 3.71 x))   (b)
−27.8992
No (more) answers
&which(x:TIMES(4.83 −3.72 x))   (c)
−17.9676
No (more) answers
&which(x:TIMES(−1.98 −5.63 x))   (d)
11.1474
No (more) answers
&.

In the second half of the examples / is the symbol we use for divide, so b/a means b divided by a. Working in the same way as we did for subtraction using **SUM**, we can say that there are three possible situations which can arise using **TIMES**:

    TIMES(a b **x**)   **TIMES**(a **x** b)   **TIMES**(**x** a b)

The first arrangement gives the straight-forward case of the product, as we have seen in the above examples. By analogy you would expect the remaining two cases to give **x** as b/a. Let's see if that's the way it works out with the second half of the questions.

&which(x:TIMES(x 4.27 4.98))   (e)
1.16627635
No (more) answers
&which(x:TIMES(x −5.63 1.98))   (f)
−0.351687389
No (more) answers
&which(x:TIMES(x −11.82 9.18))   (g)
−0.776649746
No (more) answers
&which(x:TIMES(x −14.91 −23.62)) (h)
1.5841717
No (more) answers
&.

So, it does work in the same way as the add and subtract operations!

In (e)   **x** = 1.16627635 = 4.98/4.27
In (f)   **x** = −0.351687389 = 1.98/(−5.63)
In (g)   **x** = −0.776649746 = 9.18/(−11.82)
In (h)   **x** = 1.5841717 = −23.62/(−14.91)

Either of the expressions **TIMES**(x a b) or **TIMES**(a **x** b) when queried with the **which** command gives **x**=b/a.

4.4   Large and small numbers

You will have noticed that in the solutions to Examples 4.2 (e) and (f) above the numbers generated were not whole numbers, deliberately so, and that they were expressed to a precision of 9 significant figures. (It always seems to be division which generates the unwieldy numbers doesn't it?) The numbers in the questions were fairly uniform in nature, having about the same number of significant figures, and varying in magnitude from −23.62 up to 17.48, and none lurking too close to zero where we always find trouble.

I'm going to take some of the numbers which I used in the above examples, and leave the precision the same but vary their sizes:

&which(x:TIMES(x 4.27 0.00000498))
1.16627635E−6
No (more) answers
&which(x:TIMES(x −5.63 0.000198))
−3.51687389E−5
No (more) answers
&which(x:TIMES(x −0.00001182 9.18))
−776649.746
No (more) answers
&which(x:TIMES(x −0.0000001491 −2362))
1.5841717E10
No (more) answers
&.

By comparing the results of these with the previous calculations you will see that the precision of the answers is exactly the same as before, 116627635, 351687389, 776649746 and 15841717, but the magnitude, as shown by the position of the decimal point, has changed. It has also generated a new notation for us, involving the **E** symbol. I have also assumed in what I have said, that the numbers should be seen as having two parts: a **precision** and a **magnitude**.

The symbol **E** stands for 'multiply by 10 raised to the power of', so you could have said:

  1.5841717E10 means   1.5841717*10 raised to the power of 10
               or   1.5841717*10000000000

  1.16627635E−6 means 1.16627635*10 raised to the power of −6
            or 1.16627635*(1/1,000,000)

  −3.51687389E−5 means −3.51687389* 10 raised to the power of −5
            or −3.51687389*(1/100,000)

You can enter data into programs using the **E** notation if you wish. So, you could have asked the question in that form:

> **&which(x:TIMES(x 4.27 4.98E−6))**
> **1.16627635E−6**
> **No (more) answers**
> **&.**

This standard form of expressing numbers in two parts, the precision and exponent (E), is common in computing generally. You will have noticed that the first part of the number, the precision or accuracy part, is always expressed as a number between 1 and 10. Systems do differ particularly in how many significant figures they use to express the accuracy of a number. The Acornsoft version of micro-PROLOG which I am using expresses the magnitude to nine significant figures, as you can see from the examples above. So, for large numbers, either positive or negative, until the precision has reached almost 999999999, it will not change into **E** form. Try this out for yourself:

> **&which(x:TIMES(100000000 9.999999998 x))**
> **999999999**
> **No (more) answers**
> **&which(x:TIMES(100000000 9.999999999 x))**
> **1E9**
> **No (more) answers**
> **&.**

On the other hand if you start off with fractional numbers, 0.1 in the example below, you will find that it will express these in the **E** form automatically:

> **&which(x:TIMES(0.1 0.1 x))**
> **1E−2**
> **No (more) answers**
> **&.**

EXERCISE 4.1*

Write **which** statements to find the values of the following arithmetic expressions. I have used the computer symbols for multiplication (*) and division (/) and the **E** notation for 'raise 10 to the power of'.

(a)   382798.45 + 1987.32   (b)   7234.25E6 + 36.8942E8
(c)   9822.99 − 7194.65   (d)   9.742E−3 + 21.85E−4
(e)   1.092367E10 − 42.98

(f)   8462.37 * 9427.82   (g)   12.86E8 * 7.554E9
(h)   7944.37 / 2894.71   (i)   79.43E−4 / 21.79E7
(j)   79.43E−4 / 56.82E−7

4.5   Accuracy and the **INT** operator

4.5.1   ACCURACY

It is not the appropriate place to go into great detail about the accuracy of how numbers are represented in a computer. In question (e) in Exercise 4.1 the answer is 1.092367E10, showing that the subtraction of 42.98 has made no difference, because it is below the accuracy of how 1.092367E10 is represented in the machine.

   If you realise also that numbers are not stored in decimal but in binary form, then you must see this as another source of possible inaccuracy. For example the number 3 may have been reached by means of a calculation in the machine, and may be stored at 2.99999999 or 3.00000001 not as 3.00000000 exactly. If now we use this number for another calculation, e.g. 3 squared (3*3) then the answer will certainly not be represented as exactly 9.00000000, but possibly as 8.99999999 or 9.00000001. Sometimes it is important to ensure that the result of a calculation is represented by a whole number, hence the use of the **INT** operator.

4.5.2   **INT** OPERATOR

To find the whole number part of a number you can use the **INT** operator in a **which** statement in the following way:

       &which(x:3.51 INT x)
       3
       No (more) answers
       &which(x:3567.92 INT x)
       3567
       No (more) answers
       &which(x: −3.51 INT x)
       −4
       No (more) answers
       &which(x: −3567.92 INT x)
       −3568
       No (more) answers
       &.

The effect of the **INT** operator is to ignore the fractional part of the number — in fact it chops off the fractional part leaving you with the next lowest whole number. This is easy to follow for positive numbers: in the examples above 3.51 is chopped to 3, and 3567.92 is chopped to 3567. For negative numbers you may have to pause for thought. Remember the 'number line':

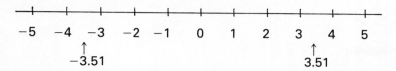

So, if the effect is to reduce the number to the next lowest whole number, then −3.51 will be chopped down to −4, and much lower down the number line −3567.92 will be reduced to −3568. On the number line principle 'lower down' means move to the left down the line.

An editorial point worth noting here is that in

    &which(x: −3.51 INT x)

the space between the : and the − is essential. If you leave out the space you get an error message which leads you to conclude that the machine is trying to read **:−3.51** as a hyphenated word! When positive numbers are used, however, micro-PROLOG is forgiving if you omit the space.

You can also use **INT** in a unary sentence with the **is** command:

    &is(22 INT)
    YES
    &is(22.17 INT)
    NO
    &.

So the two ways in which **INT** can be used may be summarised:

    which(x: a INT x)   and   **is(a INT)**

4.6   The **LESS** and **EQ** operators and combining expressions

These two operators extend our arithmetic vocabulary. They are usually found in more complex combinations of expressions. You will follow how they work if I just show a few examples:

    &is(3.51 EQ 3)
    NO
    &is(3 EQ 3)
    YES
    &is(3.51 LESS 3)
    NO
    &is(3 LESS 3.51)
    YES
    &.

So the syntax is:

    is(a **EQ** b)   and   **is**(a **LESS** b)

You can ask simple questions using the **which** command but they do not get you very far:

>   **&which(x:x EQ 3)**
>   **3**
>   **No (more) answers**
>   **&.**

To substitute **LESS** for **EQ** in the last query just gets you an error message. However, we will use these new found operators to look at the **INT** function:

>   **&is(−3 LESS −3.51)**
>   **NO**
>   **&is(−4 LESS −3.51)**
>   **YES**
>   **&.**

You can combine these sentences about numbers using the **and** operator. In this case you could be more explicit about the integer value of −3.51 being −4:

>   **&is(−3.51 INT x and x EQ −4)**
>   **YES**
>   **&.**

If you wished to find the whole number or integer solution to a division, you could proceed:

>   **&which(x y:TIMES(x 6 43) and x INT y))**
>   **7.16666667 7**
>   **No (more) answers**
>   **&which(xy:SUM(12.72 6.43 x) and x INT y))**
>   **19.15 19**
>   **No (more) answers**
>   **&.**

You can also combine **TIMES** and **SUM** expressions:

>   **&which(x y:TIMES(3 4 x) and SUM(x 5 y))**
>   **12 17**
>   **No (more) answers**
>   **&.**

It is important to note that the combination of expressions has been evaluated in a particular sequence. For example, in the last expression the **x** in **TIMES(3 4 x)** must have been calculated first, and then that value passed on to **SUM(x 5 y)**, otherwise you would have got an error message saying 'too many variables' about **SUM(x 5 y)**. In other words the combined expressions are evaluated from left to right within the **which** bracket. This is maybe what you would expect, but what you expect is not always what you get in computing.

Let's go back and look at strings for a moment. You will remember we said that all characters are represented by numbers inside the machine. We certainly do not wish to add or multiply strings of characters, but we may wish to know if strings are equal. Further as the ASCII code for the letters of the alphabet is in ascending numerical order — e.g. A is 65, B is 66, C is 67 etc., and a is 97, b is 98, c is 99 and so on — you can use the **LESS** operator to look at alphabetical order:

>   **&is(JONES LESS SMITH)**
>   **YES**
>   **&is(JONES LESS Jones)**
>   **YES**
>   **&is(JONES EQ Jones)**
>   **NO**
>   **&is(JONES LESS DAVIES)**
>   **NO**
>   **&.**

We will use this feature to put facts into alphabetical order later in the book, and to search through an ordered file looking for items of data.

EXERCISE 4.2*

(a)   Write PROLOG statements to find the integer value of the following expressions.

  (i)   3742.62 + 976.83
 (ii)   493.22 * 63.82
(iii)   1.04E5 * 9.63E3
(iv)   7.983E12 / 5.843E8

(b)   What is the result if you

  (i)   add 35 to −83 and multiply the result by 14, and
 (ii)   multiply 35 by 1.80 and add the result to 32.

(c)   Is 279 * 5 exactly divisible by 15?

(d)   Is 68.42 / 749 less than 0.1?

(e)   Write a rule **lesseq** to find whether a number is 'less than or equal to another'. In the same way write a rule for **greatereq**.

Summary

1   **SUM**(a b a+b)
  which(x:SUM(a b x))   gives x=a+b
  which(x:SUM(x a b))   gives x=b−a
  which(x:SUM(a x b))   gives x=b−a

2   **TIMES**(a b a*b)
  which(x:TIMES(a b x))   gives x=a*b
  which(x:TIMES(x a b))   gives x=b/a
  which(x:TIMES(a x b))   gives x=b/a

3   The Normal Form of a large or small number is aEb, where:
  a is a number between 1 and 10
  Eb means 'multiply by 10 raised to the power of b';
  b is a number in the range −32 to +32.

4 is(a INT)   is true if **a** is an integer
   which(x:a INT x) gives x=integer value of a

5 is(a EQ b)   is true if a=b

   is(a LESS b)   is true if a<b

   EQ and **LESS** are valid comparators for strings as well as numbers.

5

Lists and data-bases

5.1 Introduction

The idea of a **list** arises naturally from the way in which we try to give a sense of order and tidiness to the data which we use. Even before you go to work each day, it is quite likely that you will have used a list in some form or other. You may have made out a shopping list, or list of jobs to be done that day, or have consulted a telephone directory or train time-table, or looked at a newspaper list of horses running in a race, players in a team, or television programmes for the day; all of which involved writing down or reading from an ordered collection of facts and figures, or what you would refer to in everyday terms as a list. The computing use of the term is only just slightly more specialised than the way in which we use it in everyday language.

In our working and learning activities lists abound in various shapes and sizes. As a manager you may have before you a list of staff who are absent that day, a list of meetings, an agenda list of items to be discussed at those meetings, details of last week's sales figures, or the half year's statement of accounts, and so on. As a teacher you may be consulting a reference book for details of the physical properties of certain materials, or a list of synonyms for a particular word, or a table listing the balance of payments figures for the last decade, or have just consulted a room time-table or list of marks in a mark book, and so on. Every shop, factory or commercial concern will have detailed lists of staff, raw materials and equipment, detailed schedules of work to be done — the list is endless, if you will excuse the pun! In using this book you will probably already have consulted the list of contents and the index.

Such bodies of facts and figures are usually referred to in computing jargon as **data-bases**. Micro-PROLOG is a data-base and query language, and so you would expect 'lists' to be a very important topic of study in this language, and so it is. In normal commercial computing terms the term data-base usually refers to a body of data with a very clearly defined and regular structure. Because micro-PROLOG is so suited to processing data-bases which are both regular and irregular in structure, I feel that micro-PROLOG's capability of handling bases with traditional regular structures has to some extent been neglected in other introductory texts. I shall try to rectify this omission by looking at examples in some detail, using micro-PROLOG methods but pointing out the similarities between these and traditional modes of interrogation.

5.2 Closed lists

To start with you should think of a list as a sequence of facts separated by spaces, and enclosed in brackets. A **closed** list is one in which the number of facts is known and held constant, in contrast to an **open** list whose length is not known and may vary. A list is just a way of collecting a group of related facts, or names of objects, together in one package, rather than entering them separately as individual items of data.

In micro-PROLOG a list of the four longest rivers in the British Isles would look like:

(Severn Thames Trent Gt-Ouse)

It is just the names of the four rivers separated by spaces and enclosed in brackets as defined above. The only seeming technicality is the 'Gt' standing for 'Great' and the - binding this abbreviation to the word 'Ouse' to keep it as one fact. You can put this collective fact into the usual sentence form of

fact	relationship	fact
Britain	has-rivers	(Severn Thames Trent Gt-Ouse)

where the whole list is seen as one fact, an entity in its own right. To enter this sentence into micro-PROLOG's data-base you use the command **add**, as previously:

&add(Britain has-rivers (Severn Thames Trent Gt-Ouse))
&.

taking care to get the correct number of right-hand closing brackets.

You could, of course, have entered the same data into the base as separate items of data:

&accept river-in
river-in(Britain Severn)
river-in(Britain Thames)
river-in(Britain Trent)
river-in(Britain Gt-Ouse)
&.

But these would have to be seen and used as four separate data sentences, rather than as a single data sentence. Returning to the list sentence you will get the feeling that the system sees the list as a single entity by the following interaction:

&list has-rivers
Britain has-rivers (Severn Thames Trent Gt-Ouse)
&.

just to show what is in the data-base, and then the query:

&which(x y:x has-rivers y)
Britain (Severn Thames Trent Gt-Ouse)
No (more) answers
&.

Note carefully that the system sees **x** as a single fact, but **y** as a set of facts collected into one entity — a list — and thus **y** is enclosed in brackets, while **x** is not.

On the other hand the two queries:

&is(Britain has-rivers Thames)
NO
&.

followed by:

&is(Britain has-rivers (Thames))
NO
&.

show that you cannot easily get at individual items of the list if you do not pose the query using the same pattern as the list which you entered. If you do use the same pattern, the list with four items, micro-PROLOG responds predictably:

&is(Britain has-rivers (x1 Thames x2 x3))
YES
&.

To be able to ask such a question you would have to know that Thames is the second longest river, or just that it occupies the second position in the list, which, if you did, would imply that you know that it is in the list anyway, so why ask the question in the first place? Later we will spend some time in working out a rule which will search through a list to find whether an element belongs to the list or not, but not yet.

If you knew that there were four rivers named in the list you could ask the question in the form:

&which(x1 x2 x3:Britain has-rivers (x1 x2 x3 x4))
Severn Thames Trent Gt-Ouse
No (more) answers
&.

Or if you wished to find which river is third in the list you could ask the question in the general form:

&which(x:Britain has-rivers (x1 x2 x x3))
Trent
No (more) answers
&.

So far we have looked at sentences with the form:

fact   relationship   list

Let's extend this idea a little and now consider sentences with the form:

list   relationship   list

My favourite Junior Encyclopedia summarises the lives of writers, poets and dramatists in the following rather cryptic way:

Shakespeare William (1564–1616), poet and dramatist, Hamlet

You could translate these facts into the form of lists:

&add((Shakespeare William) key-facts ("1564–1616" poet
1dramatist Hamlet))
&.

Now if you ask the question:

&which(x y:x key-facts y)
(Shakespeare William) ("1564–1616" poet dramatist Hamlet)
No (more) answers
&.

you can see clearly that **x** and **y** are the two lists, whereas you could pick out all of the items in the lists as individual elements with the more detailed query:

> **&which(x1 x2 x3 x4 x5 x6:(x1 x2) key-facts (x3 x4 x5 x6))**
> **Shakespeare William "1564–1616" poet dramatist Hamlet**
> **No (more) answers**
> **&.**

If, on the other hand, you just wished to pick out the surname and when he lived, you could ask:

> **&which(x y:(x x1) key-facts (y x2 x3 x4))**
> **Shakespeare "1564–1616"**
> **No (more) answers**
> **&.**

You may protest that this example is a little contrived because you could easily have entered the name as a single item 'Shakespeare-William', as we did earlier in the book. That is true. But another entry in the same sort of data-base would have looked equally contrived as 'Shaw-George-Bernard'.

You may have wondered about why the dates are entered **"1564–1616"** in quotes, and probably guessed the answer which is if you enter this fact as 1564–1616, micro-PROLOG sees it as two numeric facts 1564 and −1616, and treats them as separate numbers suitable for calculations. When they are enclosed in quotes, however, they are interpreted as just a single string of characters.

EXERCISE 5.1*

We have used several data-bases so far in this book. The facts in all of them could have been more efficiently stored using lists, than in their individual sentence form. Go back to the (a) ROYAL, (b) CITIES, (c) ANIMALS data-bases and express the facts in them in the form of lists.

5.3   Traditional data-bases

As I said earlier in the chapter, in usual computing parlance a data-base is seen as a body of facts and figures which is organised in a specific way, traditionally seen to be set out on paper in clearly defined rows and columns, with each column containing facts of a common type, and each row representing an individual collection of data. I will introduce some of the ideas of traditional data-bases through an example, and then go into the ideas more thoroughly later.

EXAMPLE 5.1

A simple, and probably the most consulted, data-base is the telephone directory. Consider each entry in the directory as a list, and the whole directory as a collection of such lists, or if you like as a list of lists.

The first two entries in my personal directory may look like:

Radnor	Peter	Maidstone	0622	49721
Flewitt	Ray	Swanley	87	67251

To save space in the book I will not include the addresses for these entries, but obviously it would be convenient in real life to do so. As shown above, each entry in the directory relates to one person, and contains five facts: surname, first name, the name of the exchange, followed by its dialling code from my home, and then finally by the number on that exchange. In what I have been calling the 'traditional' data-base the whole directory would appear as just a collection of these rows of facts, divided into columns: one for the surname, the next for first name and so on.

In traditional terminology each row would be called a **record**, each fact in that row a **field**, and the whole collection of records a **file**. Asking questions of a file is usually referred to, rather grandly, as **interrogation**.

My micro-PROLOG TELE data-base or file has a slightly different form, but the similarities are obvious:

> **&list all**
> **(Radnor Peter) tele-no (Maidstone "0622" 49721)**
> **(Flewitt Ray) tele-no (Swanley "87" 67251)**
> **(Connors Rita) tele-no (London "01" 4629972)**
> **(Howson Hetty) tele-no (London "01" 2632283)**
> **(Adney Michael) tele-no (Orpington "0689" 45640)**
> **(Pogsen Peter) tele-no (Tamworth "0827" 75932)**
> **(Smith Alison) tele-no (Tonbridge "0732" 56432)**
> **(Teague Montagu) tele-no (Edenbridge "0732" 42961)**
> **&.**

The TELE data-base

The data was entered using the **accept** command:

> **&accept tele-no**
> **tele-no((Radnor Peter) (Maidstone "0622" 49721))**
> . . . etc. . . .

The exchange dialling codes were entered in quotes as shown — e.g. **"0622"** — because if they are entered as numbers beginning with 0, then the 0 is dropped when the data-base is listed, which would be very misleading for dialling. So the exchange code is a string, while the actual telephone number is left as a number. Even this last arrangement is not fool-proof, because most London numbers are expressed in two parts — e.g. 462 9972 or 462-9972 — which would be seen by micro-PROLOG as two separate numbers, as I have said before. So I have combined the two parts into one number. It just shows how careful you have to be in coding your data.

To look for a particular telephone number if you know the surname of the person involved is quite simple:

> **&which(Pogsen y:(Pogsen x2) tele-no y)**
> **Pogsen (Tamworth "0872" 75932)**
> **No (more) answers**
> **&.**

This would find the details for Pogsen. If you find the look of this query rather inelegant, then you could ask it in a different way:

> **&which(x1 y:(x1 x2) tele-no y and x1 EQ Pogsen)**

would give you the same results.

The usual complaint about this type of example is that you would not use a computer program in real life, just to look up a telephone number, when obviously the usual little book in alphabetical order is far more suitable, even if the telephone is next to your micro because you use it for Micronet and/or Prestel. If, on the other hand, you cannot remember the surname of the person you wish to ring then the little book presents some difficulties, especially if there are many names in it, and if they are not entered particularly clearly and tidily. If you know that the person's first name is Peter, but have temporarily forgotten his surname, you could ask your micro-PROLOG data-base:

&**which(x1 y:(x1 Peter) tele-no y)**
Radnor (Maidstone "0622" 49721)
Pogsen (Tamworth "0827" 75932)
No (more) answers
&.

An even more difficult problem for your little book would be if you could remember only that the person lived in London, whereas in micro-PROLOG you would be in with a chance of finding it:

&**which(x1 x2 x3 x4:(x1 x2) tele-no (London x3 x4))**
Connors Rita "01" 4629972
Howson Hetty "01" 2632282
No (more) answers
&.

This has been a fairly straight-forward application of lists. The next will combine the key features of micro-PROLOG: lists, logic and rules.

EXAMPLE 5.2   THE HOLIDAY FILE

In this example the data refers to a collection of holidays which could have been compiled by a travel agent. Imagine that it is approaching the height of the holiday season, but the agent still has available a limited selection of holidays abroad. In order that he may refer to the essential details of each holiday quickly, he compiles a summary file as shown below.

Reference Number	Country	Type	Airport	Price
FR072	FR	FULL	GAT	195
FR211	FR	HALF	GAT	225
. . .	etc. . . .			

Each row or record has five items or fields, which in reverse order are: the Price per person for one week, the Airport from which the holiday leaves the UK, the Type of holiday (full- or half-board, or apartment) and the Country. If a customer thinks that after the initial enquiry a holiday may be suitable, then the Reference Number would be used to refer to another file which would contain further details of the holiday.

The data-base has 12 holiday records, which I show in micro-PROLOG form in the HOLS data-base.

&list all
FR072 refers-to (FR FULL GAT 195)
FR211 refers-to (FR HALF GAT 225)
FR832 refers-to (FR APT MAN 255)
IT225 refers-to (IT FULL LUT 210)
IT365 refers-to (IT HALF GAT 205)
IT509 refers-to (IT HALF GLAS 215)
MA078 refers-to (MAJ HALF BIRM 185)
MA147 refers-to (MAJ FULL GAT 205)
MA364 refers-to (MAJ FULL GAT 175)
SP137 refers-to (SP FULL GLAS 190)
SP481 refers-to (SP HALF GAT 170)
SP722 refers-to (SP APT GAT 190)
&.

The HOLS data-base

If a customer did not mind which country she went to but was only concerned that the holiday was half-board, the following query would find those holidays of that type in the file:

&which(x x1 x2 x3 x4:x refers-to (x1 x2 x3 x4)
1and x2 EQ HALF)
FR211 FR HALF GAT 225
IT365 IT HALF GAT 205
IT509 IT HALF GLAS 215
MA078 MAJ HALF BIRM 185
SP481 SP HALF GAT 170
No (more) answers
&.

Or if the customer wanted any holiday providing it cost less than £200, the query would be:

&which(x x1 x2 x3 x4:x refers-to (x1 x2 x3 x4)
1and x4 LESS 200)
FR072 FR FULL GAT 195
MA078 MAJ HALF BIRM 185
MA364 MAJ FULL GAT 175
SP137 SP FULL GLAS 190
SP481 SP HALF GAT 170
SP722 SP APT GAT 190
No (more) answers
&.

If the customer was more particular she could ask for a holiday which was less than £200 in price, and for which the flight left from Gatwick:

&which(x x1 x2 x3 x4:x refers-to (x1 x2 x3 x4)
1and x3 EQ GAT
1and x4 LESS 200)
FR072 FR FULL GAT 195
MA364 MAJ FULL GAT 175
SP481 SP HALF GAT 170
SR722 SP APT GAT 190
No (more) answers
&.

Yes, you are right; I could have asked the half-board and Gatwick questions in a slightly simpler way, not using **and**:

      &which(x x1 x2 x3:x refers-to (x1 x2 GAT x3))

and

      &which(x x1 x2 x3:x refers-to (x1 HALF x2 x3))

would give you roughly the same results. By using the **and** form you can leave the first line of the query intact, and with the BBC micro cursor back up to that line, copy it with the Copy key and then add the second line just containing the **and** clause.

One more refinement that we will go into in more detail when we look at interactive programs, is to add text in the output lines. In the last line above we could have said:

      &which(x half-board x1 x2 x3:x refers-to (x1 HALF x2 x3))
      FR211 half-board FR GAT 225
      IT365 half-board IT GAT 205
      IT509 half-board IT GLAS 215
      MA078 half-board MAJ BIRM 185
      SP481 half-board SP GAT 170
      No (more) answers
      &.

When we looked at the logic functions in Chapter 2 I said that there is not a straight-forward 'or' operator, and that is true. In micro-PROLOG the operator is **either** . . . **or** . . . and is used in conjunction with the **and** operator itself, in the following way. If a customer requested a holiday that was either in Spain or Majorca, but not elsewhere, the travel agent would pose the question:

      &which(x x1 x2 x3 x4:x refers-to (x1 x2 x3 x4)
      1and (either x1 EQ SP or x1 EQ MAJ))

and the resulting output would be the last six sentences of the Holiday file. The first line picks out the fields or facts that are wanted, and the second line gives the proviso that either **x1** is **SP**, or **x1** is **MAJ**. So the **and** is being used to combine the two halves of the sentence together.

If the question had been posed in the following way: 'I don't mind where I go as long as it is neither Spain nor Majorca!', then this query could have been posed by adding a **not** to the second line of the above query:

      1and not (either x1 EQ SP or x1 EQ MAJ))

The last example operated on just the one field in the record, which was denoted by the symbol **x1**. The **either** . . . **or** . . . operator can just as well control more than one field. If the request were for a value-for-money holiday, in that it had either to be full-board or cheaper than £190, then the following query would do the job:

      &which(x x1 x2 x3 x4:x refers-to (x1 x2 x3 x4)
      1and (either x2 EQ FULL or x4 LESS 190))
      FR072 FR FULL GAT 195
      IT229 IT FULL LUT 210
      MA078 MAJ HALF BIRM 185
      MA147 MAJ FULL GAT 205
      MA364 MAJ FULL GAT 175

MA364 MAJ FULL GAT 175
SP137 SP FULL GLAS 190
SP481 SP HALF GAT 170
No (more) answers
&.

Now, you will see clearly that what I said in Chapter 2 was quite accurate; the 'or' function is not quite what you would have expected if you had met the operator before. Note how the output has included the **MA364** record twice. It found it first when searching for **x2 EQ FULL** and again when looking for **x4 LESS 190**. **MA364** is the only sentence which obeys both criteria, and PROLOG has picked it out and displayed it on both occasions. **MA364** satisfies the **and** condition, where the holiday is both **FULL** and **LESS 190**. Had the **either** . . . **or** . . . operator been the pure mathematical 'or' then the record would have been output only once.

You can combine some of these queries into 'rules' which can be added to the data-base, and used as required. If the travel agent knows from experience that his most frequent requests are for either a cheap holiday, or for one which starts from Gatwick, then these could be embodied into rules, so he can get at the data more quickly when asked by the customer:

&add(x1 cheap-hol (x1 x2 x3 x4) if
1x1 refers-to (x1 x2 x3 x4) and
1x4 LESS 200)
&.

This adds a 'cheap holiday' (**cheap-hol**) rule to the data-base, which, when listed, will appear at the foot of the file as:

The HOLS file as above showing only the last record

SP722 refers-to (SP APT GAT 190)
X cheap-hol (Y Z x y) if
 X refers-to (Y Z x y) and
 y LESS 200
&.

So, if you now entered:

&which(x y:x cheap-hol y)

you will get the set of holidays with Price less than £200 which was generated above.

In the same way to anticipate those customers wanting to fly from Gatwick, the following rule could be entered:

&add(x from-Gatwick (x1 x2 x3 x4) if
1x refers-to (x1 x2 x3 x4) and
1x3 EQ GAT)
&.

This will appear below the previous rule at the foot of the HOLS data-base, as:

X from-Gatwick (Y Z x y) if
 X refers-to (Y Z x y) and
 x EQ GAT
&.

Notice again how the micro-PROLOG interpreter has taken the variables which were entered as **(x x1 x2 x3 x4)** and changed them into its own set **(X Y Z x y)**. The query:

    &which(x y:x from-Gatwick y)

would give the same set of records as was generated by the earlier question. It is now easier to ask composite questions like, 'I want a cheap holiday and must fly from Gatwick.', by using both rules in conjunction:

    &which(x y:x cheap-hol y and x from-Gatwick y)
    FR072 (FR FULL GAT 195)
    MA364 (MAJ FULL GAT 175)
    SP481 (SP HALF GAT 170)
    SP722 (SP APT GAT 190)
    No (more) answers
    &.

5.4   Last words

As you will now readily appreciate micro-PROLOG has great potential even just as a means of interrogating a traditional style data-base. It compares very favourably in its interrogating facilities with professional data-base packages which are currently available for micros.

To appreciate its power you have to experience using it for a task which is of direct interest to you. If you are a historian, even an amateur local historian, it has great potential for analysing parish records, or Domesday project material for example. As a geographer you could be interested in weather statistics. The whole question of classification in biology, as we hinted at earlier, would obviously be improved by the bulk storage of facts and figures in a data-base. Everywhere that data is expressed in the form of a list or table, this method has direct application: racing, football pools and the stock-market have more than just gambling in common!

PREAMBLE TO EXERCISE 5.2

It would obviously be of greater interest and relevance to you if you could think of your own examples at this stage. Other people's data-bases are never as immediate as your own, and those in books often seem simplistic, even rather fatuous. If an example of your own does not spring immediately to mind, or if you feel you want more practice in the methods before tackling your own problem, then try the Known Offenders data-base and its rules.

EXERCISE 5.2*

The following data-base gives details about possible offenders known to the police. The first fact gives the initials of the suspect followed by a number, this combination acting as a Reference Number which would lead on to a more detailed file about the suspect. The list part of each sentence summarises the physical characteristics of each person.

&list all
BP972 description (f 59 t h d br)
DM032 description (m 33 t m l bl)
JB855 description (m 35 m h d bl)
MT258 description (f 45 m h m br)
NS137 description (f 24 t l d br)
PE652 description (m 17 t l l bl)
RP278 description (f 50 t h d br)
SJ993 description (m 27 s h l bl)
WA279 description (f 26 m m l br)
YF869 description (m 57 t h d br)
&.

The Known Offenders data-base

The first field of the list gives the sex (**m** or **f**) and the second the age in years. The third gives the height (**t m** or **s**) for (tall medium or short), and the fourth gives the weight (**h m** or **l**) for (heavy medium or light). The last two elements give colour of hair (**d l** or **m**) for (dark light or medium), and colour of eyes (**br** or **bl**) for (brown or blue).

Yes, it is a fairly simplistic method of coding the data, and is meant to represent a fairly light-weight approach to what is a serious problem, fraught with social and moral questions — I realise. It does give us the opportunity to ask those sorts of questions which occur in books and television programmes about criminal activities, where a witness has had only a fleeting glimpse of a suspect and can say, 'He was oldish, tall and of fairly heavy build', giving only a vague and very general description.

Write queries in PROLOG to answer the following questions:

(a)   Pick out just the female suspects.
(b)   Pick out the 'older' suspects — e.g. those over 40 (?!).
(c)   Find those records for 'older' females.
(d)   Find the tall suspects.
(e)   Find the female suspects who are tall and over 40.
(f)   Find the records for those suspects who would satisfy the following descriptions:
   (i)   'I only had time to notice that he had blue eyes and blond hair!'
   (ii)   'He was oldish, tall and of fairly heavy build!'
(g)   Make up a rule for 'large' suspects — e.g. those who are both tall and heavily built.
(h)   Make up a rule for 'dark' suspects — e.g. those who have both dark hair and brown eyes.
(i)   Use these two rules to find the large and dark suspects.

EXERCISE 5.3

I do not include all of the data for this exercise at this point, but you will find my version in the Answers, and further I would suggest that you will see more relevance in the details if they relate to the types of property in area in which you live.

This is yet another example from the High Street, an estate agent's file, and has proved to be a very successful classroom exercise in BASIC programming and in using the data-base package dBASEII.

Reference Number	Name of the Area	Type of Property	Bedrooms	Reception Rooms	Garages	Garden	Price
WW14	West Wickham	D	3	2	0	L	70000
Cl23	Chislehurst	D	5	3	2	M	210000
. . .	etc. . . .						

For Type of Property the codes I used were (D S T M B F) for (Detached Semi-detached Terraced Maisonette Bungalow Flat).

The Rooms were just digits, as was the Garage with **0** indicating 'none'.

The Gardens were (L M S N) for (Large Medium Small None)

The Price must be entered as a number without a comma, and of course no £ sign.

If you enter about 20 houses into the data-base from about five different areas, then you can generate a variety of meaningful questions, along the following lines — 'I want a house in Bexley with a large garden!', 'We must have bungalow with a large garden, and at least three bedrooms!', 'It must be detached with four bedrooms and be less than £90000!'. I leave the actual queries to you but you will find my approach in the Answers.

Summary

1 A **list** is a sequence of facts, or names of objects, separated by spaces and enclosed in brackets.

2 A **closed list** is one in which the number of items in the list is fixed and known before processing starts.

3 Lists may occur in PROLOG sentences with the forms:

fact   relationship   list

list   relationship   list

4 The traditional data-base form was seen as a collection of lists, where each list is referred to as a **record**, and each item in that list as a **field**. The whole collection of records makes up the data-base **file**. The process of querying a data-base is traditionally called **interrogation**.

5 We used the logical operators **and** and **not** to query lists, together with the comparators **EQ** and **LESS**.

6 The **either** . . . **or** . . . operator can be used in conjunction with **and** to give an output which is very similar to that which would be generated by the logical 'or' function, except that the **and** cases which are included in the 'or' are repeated in the output.

7 Text can be included in a **which** query in the following way:

&which(variables text variables: . . . etc. . . .)

6
List processing

6.1 Introduction

In the last chapter we looked at closed lists, i.e. lists of a fixed known length. If your data-base consists of a body of records in the form of closed lists, then you can carry out what I referred to as traditional data-base interrogation methods using the logic operators, simply by arranging for similar items of data to be at the same position in each of the lists in your file.

It is not always easy nor appropriate to present or store data in such neat fixed packages. If we start back with the entries in the encyclopedia which we used in the last chapter, then you will readily see the difficulty:

Shakespeare William (1564–1616), poet and dramatist. Hamlet.
Wilde Oscar (1856–1900), poet, critic and dramatist. Importance of Being Ernest.

Oscar Wilde is known according to the authors of that volume on three counts, as poet, critic and dramatist, while Shakespeare is known on only two. If you wished to express these facts in data-base form then you would be faced with the problem of how many fields you have in each record, or in our case in micro-PROLOG, how many items you have in your lists. One solution is for the data-base to contain lists which are not all of the same length. If you wish to process lists whose lengths are not known beforehand, then you naturally have to allow for their having any possible length; such lists I shall refer to as **open**.

The way to process open lists is to inspect each item in the list separately one by one. The way that this is done in micro-PROLOG is to cut up the original list into successively smaller lists, until the whole list has been chopped up. This idea of seeing a list as a collection of smaller lists, rather like Russian dolls, leads us naturally to the idea of **recursion**, which is central to micro-PROLOG processing.

We will write rules for inspecting the individual items in a list, to find the number of items in it, to add up the values of the items if they are numbers, to find the largest and smallest values in the list, and so on. If the rules are written in general terms such that they apply to any list, then once the routines have been written they need never be written again. You can store them away on disk, and just call them up when you wish to do that sort of processing. During this chapter we will build up an armoury, or tool-kit of these procedures or **facilities**.

6.2 Chopping up lists

The symbol | is used to show the point of division of a list. A list which has been divided up into two parts may be shown as **(X | Y)**. Even though this indicates that the list is in two parts, the expression **(X|Y)** must still be seen as representing a complete list. I've entered a simple sentence which includes a list of the four main components of a micro-computer system. Let's get the language itself to show us what is happening!

> **&list all**
> **computer main-parts (input output processor backing-store)**
> **&.**

We can see what the above notation means by asking the question:

> **&which(X Y:computer main-parts (X|Y))**
> **input (output processor backing-store)**
> **No (more) answers**
> **&.**

The original list has been chopped into two parts **X=input**, and **Y=(output processor backing-store)**. **X** is the first item in the list, and **Y** is the remainder of the list. It is very important to grasp that **X** is a single fact, and that **Y** is a list, i.e. two different data types. **X** is not a list with one item of data. We can go on and extend these ideas:

> **&which(X Y Z:computer main-parts (X Y|Z))**
> **input output (processor backing-store)**
> **No (more) answers**
> **&.**

The **X** and **Y** now pattern-match to the first two elements of the original list, and the **Z** after the | symbol stands for the remaining list, of just two items in this case. We can say that the | sign is a way of 'partitioning' the list.

Having started this line of investigation, let's continue in case it yields up any more ideas:

> **&which(X Y Z x:computer main-parts (X Y Z|x))**
> **input output processor (backing-store)**
> **No (more) answers**
> **&which(X Y Z x y:computer main-parts (X Y Z x|y))**
> **input output processor backing-store( )**
> **No (more) answers**
> **&.**

The first of the two queries gives a predictable result, but the second does tell us something new. The question tries to match five variables **(X Y Z x y)** against what looks like a list with just four items in it. The fact that **y** is matched to **( )** is very interesting, and important to the work in the rest of the chapter. **( )** is the symbol for an **empty** list, i.e. a list with no items in it. Many of the processes in this chapter involve chopping up a list into smaller and smaller lists until only an empty list remains, thus signalling the end of the process.

6.3   To pick out the items in a list

In the partitioning of a list using the notation **(X|Y)**, we talk of **X** as being the **head** of the list, and **Y** as the **tail**. To pick out or identify each item in the list, we have to imagine the list being successively divided up into smaller and smaller lists until finally the empty list is reached.

If the original list had four items in it (a b c d) then you can imagine chopping up the list in the following way:

```
1st      a | (b c d)
2nd        b | (c d)
3rd          c | (d)
4th            d | ( )
```

Using just the idea of heads and tails, then at any stage in this procedure you can say that a particular item is either the head of the list or sub-list, or that it is in the remaining tail. So, at any stage you can say:

X is an item in the list if **X** is the head of the list

or

X is an item in the list if **X** is an item in the tail

Now you may think that you have seen a possible logical flaw in the second statement, but let's ignore that possibility for the moment and continue to turn these two sentences into PROLOG rules:

> **X item-in (Y | Z) if X EQ Y**
> **X item-in (Y | Z) if X item-in Z**

In the light of our work in the last chapter, you will see that the first of these rules can be shortened slightly to:

> **X item-in (X | Z)**

which automatically makes **X** equal to **Y**. If you enter these two rules into the machine using the **add** operator, and **list** you will see:

> **&list all**
> **X item-in (X | Y)**   rule 1
> **X item-in (Y | Z) if**   rule 2
> **   X item-in Z**
> **&.**

The following query shows that the rules do pick out the members of the list one by one:

> **&which(x:x item-in (a b c d))**
> **a**
> **b**
> **c**
> **d**
> **No (more) answers**
> **&.**

The following questions reinforce the impression that the rule is working correctly.

> **&is(c item-in (a b c d))**
> **YES**
> **&is(f item-in (a b c d))**
> **NO**
> **&.**

The question is 'How do the rules solve the problem?'. The possible flaw in the second rule is the key to the solution. The problem with:

X item-in (Y|Z) if X item-in Z

is that we have defined **item-in** in terms of **item-in**. This hardly seems reasonable, and if you are well versed in this sort of thing, you might be tempted to say that to define a relationship in terms of itself is tautological. But it is this very facility, together with micro-PROLOG's habit of **backtracking** and **retrying** its rules that gives the language its power.

If you accept two general guidelines you will find understanding the **item-in** procedure quite easy. Firstly only rule 1 is capable of generating a solution: it matches an actual value to the head **X** of the list or sub-list, and outputs it. Even at the end it is rule 1 which ends the procedure by signalling that it cannot match a head to the empty list **( )**. Secondly rule 2 is always true: there is always a tail **(Z)** for which **X** might be a member, even when the tail is **( )**.

We can see how the rule works by tracing in detail what happens when the query **which(x:x item-in (a b c))** is evaluated. Now I used the micro-PROLOG trace facility in Chapter 3, and you will recall how it generated a vast quantity of detail about the query we were then tracing. This is why I have limited the list we are searching through to only three items. Remember you have to LOAD SIMTRAC on the BBC system, and then use the **all-trace** command. The trace of this query is shown in full detail in Trace Listing 6.1. To make it easier to follow my general interpretation of what is happening I have numbered the lines, and these are the numbers which appear in brackets in the following description. You will not be able to take in all of the details of the trace in one go, but it is worth returning to it frequently until you do grasp what it all means. It is certainly worth close scrutiny.

The process starts with the query sentence, shown as **X item-in (a b c)**, being matched against rule 1 in line (3) of the trace. This match succeeds in generating a solution (4), which is output (6). Remember my first guideline above which said that an actual solution can only be generated by rule 1.

The system then backtracks and tries the same query with rule 2 at line (9). The phrase in the trace **head of 1** or **head of 2**, shows you which rule it is looking at. The match succeeds (10), as my second guideline said that it must, because the tail at this point in the process has items in it — it is not empty. The match succeeds with a solution **X item-in (b c)** to rule 2 — a solution in the form of a sentence.

Now both rules have been tried, and the solution to the second is the production of a new query (11), and the system passes this query back to rule 1 to seek a solution (13). Rule 1 makes a successful match (14), and produces a solution (15). Lines (15) and (16) are interesting, because what they are saying is that if **b** is an item in **(b c)** it is also an item in **(a b c)**, so it is a solution to the original query **X item-in (a b c)**. You can imagine that the machine has been 'stacking up' these solution sentences, just waiting for a solution in the form of a value.

The numbers in brackets **(1 1)** at the left-hand side of (15), and **(1)** at the left of (16), tell you the state of partitioning of the list. At (15) the list is in two parts, hence **(1 1)**, and at (16) back at one, hence **(1)**. You will see how useful this is as a clue to what stage the process is at, especially when the partitioning gets more detailed.

The solution **b** is output at line (17), and then the system takes the query **X item-in (b c)** on to rule 2 (20), and the match succeeds (21) because the partition **(b|(c))**, still has a non-empty tail **(c)**. So the solution to rule 2 is the new query **X item-in (c)** at (22), which is then automatically passed back to rule 1 (24) to test. Once again rule 1 produces a successful match (25), and the solution **c item-in (c)** at (26). This and the next two lines go through the logic, if **c** is an item in **(c)**, then it

LOAD SIMTRAC

(1)   **&all-trace(x:x item-in (a b c))**
(2)   **(1) : X item-in (a b c) trace?y**
(3)   **matching (1) : X item-in (a b c) with head of 1 : Y item-in (Y | Z)**
(4)   **match succeeds: a item-in (a b c)**
(5)   **(1) solved : a item-in (a b c)**
(6)   **a**
(7)   **backtracking . . .**
(8)   **retrying (1)**
(9)   **matching (1) : X item-in (a b c) with head of 2 : Y item-in (Z | x)**
(10)   **match succeeds: X item-in (a b c)**
(11)   **new query : X item-in (b c)**
(12)   **(1 1) : X item-in (b c) trace?y**
(13)   **matching (1 1) : X item-in (b c) with head of 1 : Y item-in (Y | Z)**
(14)   **match succeeds: b item-in (b c)**
(15)   **(1 1) solved : b item-in (b c)**
(16)   **(1) solved : b item-in (a b c)**
(17)   **b**
(18)   **backtracking . . .**
(19)   **retrying (1 1)**
(20)   **matching (1 1) : X item-in (b c) with head of 2 : Y item-in (Y | x)**
(21)   **match succeeds: X item-in (b c)**
(22)   **new query : X item-in (c)**
(23)   **(1 1 1) : X item-in (c) trace?y**
(24)   **matching (1 1 1) : X item-in (c) with head of 1 : Y item-in (Y | Z)**
(25)   **match succeeds: c item-in (c)**
(26)   **(1 1 1) solved : c item-in (c)**
(27)   **(1 1) solved : c item-in (b c)**
(28)   **(1) solved : c item-in (a b c)**
(29)   **c**
(30)   **backtracking . . .**
(31)   **retrying (1 1 1)**
(32)   **matching (1 1 1) : X item-in (c) with head of 2 : Y item-in (Z | x)**
(33)   **match succeeds: X item-in (c)**
(34)   **new query : X item-in ( )**
(35)   **(1 1 1 1) : X item-in ( ) trace?y**
        matching (1 1 1 1) : X item-in ( ) with head of 1 : Y item-in (Y | Z)
            match fails
        matching (1 1 1 1) : X item-in ( ) with head of 2 : Y item-in (Z | x)
            match fails
        (1 1 1 1) failing : X item-in ( )
        retrying (1 1 1)
        (1 1 1) failing : X item-in (c)
        retrying (1 1)
        (1 1) failing : X item-in (b c)
        retrying (1)
        (1) failing : X item-in (a b c)
        No (more) answers
        &.

Trace Listing 6.1

is an item in **(b c)** (27), and in turn an item in **(a b c)** (28). This solution is output at line (29). Here we have that stacking up process again. Note how the **(1 1 1)**, **(1 1)** and **(1)** show the degree of partitioning from (26) to (28).

The system continues by backtracking to rule 2, to look for a match for **(c|( ))** (32), which succeeds at (33) by producing the new query **X item-in ( )** at (34). At this point I stop the line-by-line commentary, but you can see that when this query is passed back to rule 1 it fails, and the whole procedure stops eventually with **No (more) answers**.

The procedure can be summarised as follows. Rule 1 produces a solution which is an actual value, **X** the head of the list **(X|Y)**. Rule 2 produces a solution in the form of a sentence, which the backtracking and retrying facilities of the language pass back to rule 1 to re-test. We can say then that the outcome of rule 2 is a call to retry rule 1 with a new query.

6.4   Recursion

The process which we have just looked at in detail is an example of **recursion**. A dictionary definition of recursion is 'going back or returning'. A rule or definition which goes back on itself is called **recursive**. In the above example rule 2 was the recursive rule, **item-in** defined in terms of itself. Micro-PROLOG's backtracking and retrying facilities assist the process and make it a naturally recursive language. Some languages are not at all recursive — e.g. BASIC — and some tasks which are very difficult to perform in these languages, come very naturally to micro-PROLOG.

I will try to give some useful guidelines about recursion, later in the book, when you have had the experience of seeing it in use in several examples. Watch out for some points from now on. A recursive rule must have associated with it a non-recursive one (rule 1 above), to stop the process of recursion going on for ever. The second point worth noting is that if you depict the recursive rule as

    object 1   relationship   object 2   if

           object 3   relationship   object 4   and

           conditions

then usually you have to look for a relationship between objects 1 and 3, and objects 2 and 4. Keep these broad generalisations in mind when we continue with list processing in the next section.

First let's see how we can use **item-in** in a few simple exercises. Try to do the examples before looking at my solutions. The answers to the exercises are at the back of the book. In all cases it is assumed that the program **item-in** is in the memory of the machine.

EXAMPLE 6.1

(a)   Which letters in the name 'joe' are also found in the name 'eddy'?

      &which(x:x item-in (j o e) and
      1x item-in (e d d y))
      e
      No (more) answers
      &.

(b)   Which numbers in the list of numbers 8 13 11 14 9 6 10 12, have values less than 10?

> **&which(x:x item-in (8 13 11 14 9 6 10 12) and**
> **1x LESS 10)**
> **8**
> **9**
> **6**
> **No (more) answers**
> **&.**

(c)   Pick out the integers (whole numbers) in the list of numbers 9.3 6.8 9 10.2 10 8.7 6 5.2.

> **&which(x:x item-in (9.3 6.8 9 10.2 10 8.7 6 5.2) and**
> **1x INT)**
> **9**
> **10**
> **6**
> **&.**

EXERCISE 6.1*

(a)   Pick out the vowels in the word 'recursion'.
(b)   Which numbers in the following list 8 13 11 14 9 6 10 12 are even?
(c)   Find the negative numbers in the list 2.37 −4.12 3.96 −2.21 −0.17 1.98.
(d)   Find the squares of the numbers in the list 3 7 5 11 9 14.
(e)   Subtract 3 from each item in the list for (d).
(f)   Change the following list of temperatures in degrees Centigrade (Celsius) (16 19 21 17 14) into degrees Fahrenheit. (What introductory programming book worth its salt does not have this example somewhere between its covers?) The formula is $F = \frac{9}{5}C + 32$.

6.5   List processing

Using **item-in** to pick out the items in a list was our first list processing program. The rest of the chapter is concerned with similar, and related, list processing operations. The first two are very similar in nature and are designed to count the number of items in a list, and to add up their values, if they are numbers of course, to find the total of the list. These are two obviously important processes if we are interested in performing simple statistical calculations on numbers. The last function which we will consider is concerned with sticking two lists together — **appending** them.

   The first half of the chapter left us with two main weapons: the ability to partition lists, and recursion. Most of the following routines will involve this 'recursive chopping up of lists'. The end of a procedure was marked by our chopping up the list until we were left with just an empty list. So with this clear end in view we have two other considerations: to associate a value with this end point; and to make up a rule which relates each item in the list to its neighbour during the chopping up process. Let's see how far these guidelines will take us.

6.5.1   COUNTING THE ITEMS IN A LIST

In many applications you need to know the number of items in a list, so this is certainly not just an academic exercise. You have also known how to count since early childhood: you start with a number 1 (say) at the beginning of a list, and each time an item is accounted for you add 1 to the previously reached total. So, at any point in the item counting process, you can say that if the count up to that item is x, then the count at the next item will be given by Z, where Z=x+1, or in micro-PROLOG terms **SUM(x 1 Z)**.

Most counting processes start at 1, but remembering what we said about the chopping up process ending with an empty list, you should be willing to accept one fairly certain fact, and that is that the number of items in an empty list will be zero. So, you can associate the value 0 with **( )**, and can proceed to translate the English phrase 'the number of items in an empty list is zero' into a micro-PROLOG rule:

( ) count-is 0

where **count-is** is the name I have given to this relationship.

Now imagine that you are in the middle of the counting process, and your count so far is x for a list Y, then from what we said above the length of the list formed by adding one item to Y, will give a list count of Z where Z=x+1. How can you add an item to Y? The only way you know how, is to treat Y as the tail of a list, and add one more element (X) to it as a new head.

If the state is	**Y count-is x**
then if an element X is added to Y	**(X|Y) count-is Z**
where	**SUM(x 1 Z)**

You can now turn this into a micro-PROLOG rule:

(X\|Y) count-is Z if Y count-is x and SUM(x 1 Z)

Let's put the two sentences together, and **add** them into the data-base, and see if together they do the job:

```
&list all
( ) count-is 0                    rule 1
(X|Y) count-is Z if
      Y count-is x and            rule 2
      SUM(x 1 Z)
&which(x: (a b c d e) count-is x)

5
No (more) answers
&.
```

So, it does seem to work, but quite how does it do it? The difference between the explanation I gave to set up rule 2, in the text above, and rule 2 in the PROLOG program, is that my explanation assumed that **x** was known somehow, and so we could add 1 to it to get **Z**. But when the rule is evaluated initially there are no values for **x** and **Z**.

When the interpreter starts to process this program it passes through rule 1 because the target list **(a b c d e)** is not empty, and on to rule 2. It matches the target list against **(X\|Y) count-is Z** provided that **Y count-is x**. Here we have the same situation as we met in the **item-in** program, the solution to the rule is an expression **Y count-is x**, which is now passed back to rule 1 and then again on to rule 2. So the tail **Y** of **(X|Y)** has now been passed back to rule **2**, which promptly finds a new solution by passing the tail of **Y** back to rule **2**, and so on and so on, until the tail of **Y** is the empty list **( )**. This is the familiar list head-chopping process.

When **Y** becomes the empty list rule 1 comes into play and assigns the value 0 to the **x** of **count-is x**, and all of the solution sentences which have earlier been produced by rule 2 and stored away, are evaluated one by one. You will recall this stacking up process from the trace of **item-in**.

Now I hope you find this explanation credible, hopefully crystal clear. If you do not, what can you do about it? Well you could resort to tracing the solution with SIMTRAC, with all that that entails. Certainly I cannot devote pages of the book to trace print-outs, but there is a technique which you could use which may help your understanding of what is going on.

6.5.2   TRACING WITH **PP**

The characters **P** and **PP** are used in PROLOG to summon up print procedures. I will show how they can be used interactively to make programs more attractive later on in the book. At present I am concerned to use them to make the programs speak for themselves as it were, to trace what is happening at critical points in the programs.

The general way in which **P** and **PP** are used is:

    P(text or variables)   or   **PP**(text or variables)

You can print the message 'Here is rule 1' on the screen in the following way:

    &is(PP(Here is rule 1))
    Here is rule 1
    YES
    &.

If, on the other hand, you said:

    &is(P(Here is rule 1))
    Here is rule 1YES
    &.

So, you can see that the difference between **P** and **PP** is only that **PP** not only prints out on the screen the text enclosed in the brackets, but it also moves you to the left-hand side of the next new line. **P** on its own prints out the message, but leaves you at the next point on the same line for the next message from the machine. More technically, **PP** involves a 'carriage return' followed by a 'line-feed'.

Using **P** and **PP** in **is** and **which** queries may seem a bit contrived because they are not really queries at all, but their use is quite logical if you assume that **P** or **PP**(text or variables) are sentences which are true under all conditions.

What I have done then is to add the sentence **PP(rule 1)** to the end of rule 1, and **PP(rule 2 X Y Z x)** to the end of rule 2. There are no variables in rule 1, but the purpose of **PP(rule 2 X Y Z x)** is to show that the program is in the process of evaluating that rule, and to print out the value of the variables in the rule. So that I can refer to the rule separately, and store it on disk under a different name from **count-is**, I have called the relationship **pcount-is** — print with **count-is**.

The listing of this new rule (Listing 6.2) shows how the print sentences are added into the program using the **if** and **and** conjunctions:

```
&list pcount-is
() pcount-is 0 if
      rule1 PP
(X|Y) pcount-is Z if
      Y pcount-is x and
      SUM(x 1 Z) and
      PP (rule2 X Y Z x)
&which(x: (p r o l o g) pcount-is x)
rule1
rule2 g () 1 0
rule2 o (g) 2 1
rule2 l (o g) 3 2
rule2 o (l o g) 4 3
rule2 r (o l o g) 5 4
rule2 p (r o l o g) 6 5
6
No (more) answers
&.
```

Listing 6.2

Table 6.1

Head X	Tail Y	Current count Z	Previous count x
g	()	1	0
o	(g)	2	1
l	(o g)	3	2
o	(l o g)	4	3
r	(o l o g)	5	4
p	(r o l o g)	6	5

I have laid out the results in Table 6.1 to give you a clearer picture of what is happening. The process applies only to the evaluation cycle of rule 2, but if you ignore the **Z** and **x** columns which are doing the counting, you can get a pretty good idea of the head chopping sequence by reading from bottom to top of the head and tail columns. The first time through rule 2

(X|Y) becomes	**(p|(r o l o g))**
the next time	**(r|(o l o g))**
and so on,	
until finally	**(g|())**

When the chopping process finally gives the tail as ( ), then the evaluation process starts with **x=0** after passing through rule 1, which is the first line of the **PP** print-out under the query, and then on to the build up sequence of the list with the tail increasing by one item each time, and **Z** increasing from **1** to **6**.

The **PP** or Pretty Print trace does not give so much detail as the full trace with SIMTRAC, but it does give a lot of information about what the process is doing, is a lot easier to read, and in this case does give enough evidence, I think, to support my description of the last section, about how **count-is** works.

Let's backtrack ourselves and see how the technique would have helped us in the understanding of **item-in**; in the same way I have re-named the program **pitem-in** — see Listing 6.3.

```
&list pitem-in
X pitem-in (X | Y) if
      PP (rule1 X Y)
X pitem-in (Y | Z) if
      X pitem-in Z and
      PP (rule2 X Y Z)
&which(x:x pitem-in (a b c))
rule1 a (b c)
a
rule1 b (c)
rule2 b a (b c)
b
rule1 c ( )
rule2 c b (c)
rule2 c a (b c)
c
No (more) answers
&.
```

Listing 6.3

An interesting exercise is to compare this print-out with the trace in Trace Listing 6.1, and make sure that you can identify the lines in the trace which correspond to the lines printed out above.

6.5.3   ADDING UP THE VALUES OF THE ITEMS

Adding up the values in a list is the most frequent start to any statistical analysis. The **count-is** program needs only one modification to change it into a **total-is** program. The logical process is almost the same as before. See if you can spot the change needed before you look through the program below.

Yes, I expect you saw it! All you have to do is to add the head of each sub-list (**X** rather than 1) to **x** to make **Z**=**x**+**X**, to give you the running total through the list. So the program for **total-is** is as shown below, and followed by a query — see the program and run given in Listing 6.4.

```
&list total-is
( ) total-is 0
(X | Y) total-is Z if
      Y total-is x and
      SUM(x X Z)
&which(x:(1 2 3 4 5 6) total-is x)
21
No (more) answers
&.
```

Listing 6.4   Program and run

Just to show that it is working in the same way as I described for **count-is** I will write **ptotal-is** — see Listing 6.5.

```
&list ptotal-is
( ) ptotal-is 0 if
       rule1 PP
(X|Y) ptotal-is Z if
       Y ptotal-is x and
       SUM(x X Z) and
       PP(rule2 X Y Z x)
&which(x:(-13 4 23 17 -9) ptotal-is x)
rule1
rule2 -9 ( ) -9 0
rule2 17 (-9) 8 -9
rule2 23 (17 -9) 31 8
rule2 4 (23 17 -9) 35 31
rule2 -13 (4 23 17 -9) 22 35
22
No (more) answers
&.
```

Listing 6.5

If you keep clearly in mind that the variables which are being printed out are:

head   tail   current total   previous total

then you should have no difficulty in reading how the program carries out its task.

EXAMPLE 6.2

Use **total-is** and **count-is** to find the total, count and arithmetic mean of a list of numbers. As before you should treat this as an exercise to try yourself first before looking at the solution.

In two stages the solution looks like:

```
&which(x y:(1 2 3 4 5 6) count-is x and
1(1 2 3 4 5 6) total-is y)
6 21
No (more) answers
&which(x y z:(1 2 3 4 5 6) count-is x and
1(1 2 3 4 5 6) total-is y and
1TIMES(z x y))
6 21 3.5
No (more) answers
&.
```

6.5.4   APPENDING TWO LISTS

Having now spent several pages describing how to chop up lists into smaller sub-lists, we are now going to spend some time considering how to combine two lists into one longer list. The importance of being able to do this is fairly apparent, for it is quite likely that you may have collected data on a particular subject on different occasions, and have stored them as separate lists, but now you may wish to join the two lists together to form a larger data-base of all the relevant facts.

The aim of the **append-to** program can be stated quite simply: you start with two lists, **(a b c)** and **(d e)** for example, and after the **append-to** process you end up with one list **(a b c d e)**. Remember that the expression **(X|Y)**, though showing a partition, does depict a single list. The way that it is done is shown in Table 6.2.

Table 6.2

First list head	tail	Second list	Appended tail
c	( )	(d e)	(d e)
b	(c)	(d e)	(c d e)
a	(c d)	(d e)	(b c d e)

So the final list will be **(a|(b c d e))** which is **(a b c d e)**.

The general procedure is to divide the first list into head and tail, and then to append this tail to the second list. Yes, we got the same sort of tautology which we found earlier — **append** defined in terms of **append** — but we have found that this is essential to forming a recursive rule. Look back at Table 6.2 to see what this means. Well, in the first instance:

(( ) (d e)) append-to (d e)

which we can straight away turn into a general rule:

(( ) X) append-to X

or if you append a list to an empty list you end up with the original list, which all seems fairly reasonable.

If you look back at the final line of the table and follow through the following description, you will see what is happening:

If you can append the tail of first list to the second list then you can append the head and tail of the first list to the second:

    if   **(Y Z) append-to x**
    e.g.   **((b c) (d e)) append-to (b c d e)**
    then **((X|Y) Z) append-to (X|x)**
    e.g.   **((a|(b c)) (d e)) append-to (a|(b c d e))**

You can now write this as a general micro-PROLOG rule to follow the first rule above — see Listing 6.6.

```
&list append-to
(( ) X) append-to X
((X|Y) Z) append-to (X|x) if
        (Y Z) append-to x
&which(x:((a b c) (d e)) append-to x)
(a b c d e)
No (more) answers
&.
```

Listing 6.6

```
list all
(( ) X) append-to X
((X|Y) Z) append-to (X|x) if
(Y Z) append-to x
&all-trace(x:((a b) (c d)) append-to x)
(1) : ((a b) (c d)) append-to X trace?y
matching (1) : ((a b) (c d)) append-to X with head of 1 : (( ) Y) append-to Y
    match fails
matching (1) : ((a b) (c d)) append-to X with head of 2 : ((Y|Z)x) append-to Y|y)
    match succeeds: ((a b) (c d)) append-to (a   |X)
new query : ((b) (c d)) append-to X
(1 1) : ((b) (c d)) append-to X trace?y
matching (1 1) : ((b) (c d)) append-to X with head of 1 : (( ) Y) append-to Y
    match fails
matching (1 1) : ((b) (c d)) append-to X with head of 2 : ((Y|Z) x) append-to Y|y)
    match succeeds: ((b) (c d)) append-to (b|X)
new query : (( ) (c d)) append-to X
(1 1 1) : (( ) (c d)) append-to X trace?y
matching (1 1 1) : (( ) (c d)) append-to X with head of 1 : (( ) Y) append-to Y
    match succeeds: (( ) (c d)) append-to (c d)
(1 1 1) solved : (( ) (c d)) append-to (c d)
(1 1) solved : ((b) (c d)) append-to (b c d)
(1) solved : ((a b) (c d)) append-to (a b c d)
(a b c d)
backtracking . . .
retrying (1 1 1)
matching (1 1) : (( ) (c d)) append-to X with head of 2 : ((Y|Z)x) append-to Y|y)
    match fails
(1 1 1) failing : (( ) (c d)) append-to X
retrying (1 1)
(1 1) failing : ((b) (c d)) append-to X
retrying (1)
(1) failing : ((a b) (c d)) append-to X
No (more) answers
&.
```

Listing 6.7   Trace of **append-to**

Listing 6.7 shows a trace for **append-to** for the two lists **(a b)** and **(c d)**. The trace for **(a b c)** and **(d e)** proved to be too long and complicated to be worthwhile printing. Note that the third and final trace, the matching of the query with rule 1:

> **(( ) (c d)) append-to X**

triggers off the evaluation sequence and the final appended list **(a b c d)**. Compare this sequence with the output of **pappend-to** which to shown in Listing 6.8.

```
&list pappend-to
(( ) X) pappend-to X if
     rule1 PP X
((X|Y) Z) pappend-to (X|x) if
     (Y Z) pappend-to x and
     PP (rule2 X Y Z x)
```

```
&which(x:((a b) (c d)) pappend-to x)
rule1 (c d)
rule2 b ( ) (c d) (c d)
rule2 a (b) (c d) (b c d)
(a b c d)
No (more) answers
&which(x:((a b c) (d e)) pappend-to x)
rule1 (d e)
rule2 c ( ) (d e) (d e)
rule2 b (c) (d e) (c d e)
rule2 a (b c) (d e) (b c d e)
(a b c d e)
No (more) answers
&.
```

Listing 6.8

EXAMPLE 6.3

Use **append-to** to join together the two phrases 'The fifth generation' and 'will program in Prolog':

```
&which(x:((The fifth generation) (will program in Prolog))
1append-to x)
The fifth generation will program in Prolog
No (more) answers
&.
```

EXERCISE 6.2

(a)   I prefer the binary form **(X Y) append-to Z** but this rule is often expressed in the unary form **append (X Y Z)** to mean the same thing. Re-write the **append-to** rule as an **append** rule.

(b)   Use the **append-to** rule 'backwards' to divide a given list — e.g. **(a b c d e)** — into sub-lists with queries in the form:

&**which(x y:(x y) append-to (a b c d e))**

and show how the form:

&**which(x y z:(x (y|z)) append-to X)**

will do the same job as **item-in**.

(c)   Use these ideas to split a list into sub-lists or segments — e.g. cut the list of words (the sun was shining on the sea) into segments beginning with the word 'the'.

These ideas are explored further in Chapter 8.

EXERCISE 6.3

Write a rule to find the greater value of two numbers in the form of a two item list **(X Y)**, and then write a recursive rule to find the maximum value of a list of numbers containing two or more items, starting **(X Y | Z) max-is x if** . . . where **X** and **Y** are the number pair referred to above.

Write similar rules to find the minimum value of a list of numbers. Combine these rules to write a rule for the 'range' of values found in a list of numbers.

These ideas are worked through in detail in the Statistics program in Chapter 8.

Summary

1   It is possible to partition a list using the divider symbol | e.g. **(h|t)** is a list where **h** is called the **head** of the list and is a single fact, and **t** is the **tail** of the list and is itself a list.

2   A **recursive** rule is one which is defined in terms of itself. In this chapter we have written several recursive rules:

item-in finds an individual item in a list;
count-is counts the number of items in a list;
total-is adds up the values of items in a list; and
append-to joins two list together.

3   The operators **P** and **PP** allow us to print out messages and the values of variables. These operators were used widely in devising programs which trace themselves, rather than relying on the very complicated outputs from the simtrac module.

As you can see from this Summary, very few new programming operators were introduced in this chapter, but we were more concerned with devising program routines. The rest of the book follows in this same vein, so summaries will not be given from this point on.

7
Problem solving and programs

7.1   Introduction

This chapter has no grand overall theme, but does aim to revise, reinforce and extend some techniques which you have met already, and to introduce some new ideas along the way. The only way to feel really confident in the use of any programming language is to use it to solve a variety of problems — and certainly we will do that in this chapter.

In the last chapter I introduced the idea of recursion by chopping up lists into smaller lists, until the whole list had been chopped up. It seemed a fairly common-place and non-mathematical way of introducing the idea. But of course, recursion does occur quite naturally in solving a number of mathematical problems. We will start by looking at these, and if to some extent you lost the wood of recursion for the trees, now is a good time to take a fresh look at this technique.

Books on problem-solving seem often to come in two extreme types, the first where the advice given is so general that it is almost useless as a guide to solving practical problems, the other extreme is where 'common-sense' seems to be wrapped up in inexplicable psychological jargon. To give a modicum of general guidance, I will refer frequently to the main rules of practical problem solving as I see them, and you will have to judge whether they are useful to you or not.

Firstly make sure that you understand the problem. If you are not sure whether you do understand all of its possible implications, then with pencil and paper, or by using a computer if appropriate, try lots of specific examples until you feel you have grasped it in its most general sense, to embrace all possible instances. If total clarity still eludes you, then try solving simplified versions of the problem, or problems which are of a very similar type. Secondly, devise a plan for the solution, which means, in our case, write a micro-PROLOG program embodying this plan. Thirdly, carry out the plan: run the program. Lastly review the whole exercise: to ensure that it really has solved the problem, that it has been as accurate as you could possibly wish; and decide how the solution can be of use to you in your future problem solving activities.

In programming the way you devise a plan for the solution of a problem is to a large extent determined by the nature of the programming language itself. This is particularly so with micro-PROLOG. It is a very logical language, and this forces you to think logically about how to devise a program. We have been making up micro-PROLOG rules since Chapter 2, but now look at what they are telling us a little more critically.

    <sentence 1> if
        <sentence 2> and
        <sentence 3> and
        etc.

This rule is saying that <sentence 1> can be defined in terms of the conjunction of <sentence 2> and <sentence 3>; the first sentence then is a generalisation formed by the combined effects of sentences 2 and 3. So going from <sentence 1> down to the next level, which is a combination of two other sentences, we have moved from a more general rule to two less general, or more specific, rules. Later on in the program <sentence 2> may itself have been defined in terms of two other subsidiary rules, and so may <sentence 3>, and so on down the program. I have used the term 'down' rather a lot, but this process of going from the more general to the less general rule, is referred to as **top-down** programming. This method of programming is forced on us by the nature of micro-PROLOG itself. You are forced to design your programs starting from the more general instances of rules, and working 'down' towards the less general.

In this chapter as well, we will pay more attention to how information is displayed on the screen or printer, and to how we can make micro-PROLOG programs interact with the user.

7.2   Compound interest

You know this sort of problem. If you have $100 to invest, and you do so for 1 year at an interest rate of 12%, then at the end of that year it will be worth $112. Now you can take the $12 and spend it, or if you have no immediate need of it you can reinvest the whole sum $112 for a further year, after which time the total capital you have from this investment is $112 plus 12% of $112, which is $125.44. For a third year you would invest $125.44 at 12% and this would give you $140.49 to the nearest cent. If you did not fully understand the problem before we started, I hope you do now. Let's summarise it, where c_1 is the capital at the start of year 1, and c_2 the capital at the start of year 2, and so on.

$$c_2 = c_1 \times 1.12$$
$$c_3 = c_2 \times 1.12$$
$$c_4 = c_3 \times 1.12$$

etc.

or $c_4 = (((c_1 \times 1.12) \times 1.12) \times 1.12)$. You can see the 'Russian doll' arrangement of the brackets, and will realise that this is where the recursion occurs. Next year's capital will be last year's multiplied by the factor 1.12.

To solve the whole problem there are three factors which determine the final capital amount: the original capital invested, the percentage interest, and the number of years for which the investment is made. When these are entered into the correct formula, a fourth number, the final capital, will be generated.

I am here not very interested in the whole problem, because micro-PROLOG is not a number crunching language, and we might be led astray by matters of detail which will cloud the important part of the problem, viz the recursive feature. So let's concentrate on a simpler problem. Assume the initial capital is $1 and a fixed rate of interest of 15%, find the capital which will have accumulated after a given number of years. So I'm looking to form a rule of the form:

years   compounds-capital-to   amount

All of the above could be described as stage 1 of the problem solving process, understanding the problem and defining it clearly. Stage 2 is forming a plan to solve the problem, in our case writing a plan in the form of a PROLOG program. Harking back to the guidelines about recursion which I gave in the last chapter, you will remember that one of the rules must be non-recursive to stop the solution seeking process. You seek a rule like:

0   compounds-capital-to   0,

which does not seem to be particularly constructive, but certainly you can say that after one year the amount will be \$1.15, so:

1   compounds-capital-to   1.15

To make entering the program just a little easier I am going to shorten the relationship compounds-capital-to to **comp**, so my first rule is:

1 comp 1.15

In the recursive rule we said that if the rule had the form

object 1   relationship   object 2   if
            object 3   relationship   object 4   and
            conditions

then somehow object 1 must be related to object 3, and object 2 to object 4. If our recursive rule has the general terms

X comp Y if
     ...
Z comp x

then **X** is next year and **Z** is this year, so **X=Z**+1, or in micro-PROLOG terms **SUM(Z 1 X)**.

Following the same lines as the description above, we can say that next year's capital will be this year's multiplied by 1.15. So, in the above rule the condition which links **Y** and **x** will be that **Y** = **x** × 1.15, or in micro-PROLOG terms **TIMES(x 1.15 Y)**. You will now accept the following rule as being reasonable, particularly when we enter stage 3 of the problem solving procedure, that is to run the program given in Listing 7.1.

```
&list comp
1 comp 1.15
X comp Y if
        0 LESS X and
        SUM(Z 1 X) and
        Z comp x and
        TIMES(x 1.15 Y) and
        PP(X Y Z x)
&which(x:5 comp x)
2 1.3225 1 1.15
3 1.520875 2 1.3225
4 1.74900625 3 1.520875
5 2.01135719 4 1.74900625
2.01135719
No (more) answers
&.
```

Listing 7.1

There are two lines extra to those described above. You will recognise the 'trace' statement **PP(X Y Z x)**, which prints out the first four lines of the output, before the final solution **2.01135719**. There is no print statement in rule 1, so the solution for year 1 is not shown. The sentence **0 LESS X** is just a way of ensuring that the machine does not go off looking for negative years. If you do not include this sentence, you get the solution but the machine obviously goes off on a long back-track, and you finally get the message 'Error: 0 space left'. It is a fairly fundamental, and reasonable statement to include.

The query and the subsequent run of this one-relationship program constitute stage 3 of the problem-solving process. To satisfy stage 4 you will have to resort to pencil, paper and calculating machine to check through the accuracy of the output data until you are satisfied that it is doing its job. There is little to review in this particular program, because we started out by limiting the more general case to look specifically at the recursive part of the process only. If you were interested in building up a suite of programs of elementary business calculations then you would need to look at the more general cases of compound interest which I mentioned earlier. I would then question whether micro-PROLOG is the right language for that sort of application.

One final point about problem solving is that there is one important guideline which the pundits often do not mention, for devising a plan to solve a problem, and that is to decide whether you have met a similar problem before, and whether part of that previous solution could not be used to help you with your current one. You do not always have to feel obliged to re-invent the wheel every time you try to solve a 'new' problem. There is every good reason to classify solutions and their programs, and to collect them as groups of 'modules' which you can call on later to help you in your problem solving. There will be more about 'modules' in Chapter 10.

7.3   Factorials

These are numbers which occur in probability or statistical calculations, and programs for their calculation also appear in many books on micro-PROLOG produced so far because of their obvious recursive nature. The numbers arise from calculations of the number of ways possible combinations of events may occur. I will only half re-invent the wheel in this case, for I think it may be worth looking in partial detail at just one more numeric example of recursion. As soon as you feel that you understand the problem, you treat it as an exercise and try to finish off the solution and write the micro-PROLOG program.

We start off this sequence of numbers by defining factorial (1) to be 1, but from then on the sequence goes:

factorial (2) = 2 × 1   = 2
factorial (3) = 3 × 2 × 1   = 6
factorial (4) = 4 × 3 × 2 × 1 = 24

If you think about the recursion process you will see that neighbouring numbers in the sequence form the pattern:

factorial (2) = 2 × factorial (1)
factorial (3) = 3 × factorial (2)
factorial (4) = 4 × factorial (3)

and so on, so generally

factorial (n) = n × factorial (n−1)

This is stage 1 in the problem solving process over I hope — to understand the problem. To move on to stage 2 of the problem solving process, and turn these jottings into a micro-PROLOG program, you will expect the recursive rule to have the general form:

X factorial Y if

      . . .

      Z factorial x and

      . . .

Now obviously **X** and **Z** are related as before for we are just stepping one by one up through the natural numbers, so **X** = **Z** + 1 or in micro-PROLOG terms again **SUM(Z 1 X)**. **Y** will be given by seeing that it is the previous factorial **x** multiplied by the new **X**, you then have **Y** = **x** × **X**, or in micro-PROLOG terms **TIMES(X x Y)**. Accepting that factorial (1) = 1, we can write the whole rule down in one go — see Listing 7.2.

```
&list factorial
1 factorial 1
X factorial Y if
      0 LESS X and
      SUM(Z 1 X) and
      Z factorial x and
      TIMES(X x Y) and
      PP(X Y Z x)
&which(x:3 factorial x)
2 2 1 1
3 6 2 2
6
No (more) answers
&which(x:5 factorial x)
2 2 1 1
3 6 2 2
4 24 3 6
5 120 4 24
120
No (more) answers
&.
```

Listing 7.2

There is little more to say about this solution, except that you will note that I have left in the proviso that **X** shall be a positive number, **X** > 0 or **0 LESS X**. Pencil and paper checks will satisfy stage 3, that the numbers obtained from the program are correct. Finally you will review what you have done, and consider how you would use this program in a suite of modules on probability — if that is one of your interests.

EXERCISE 7.1*

If you like this sort of numeric exercise then there is another standard problem which you could try. Write a program to find the 'sum of the first n natural numbers'. What grand jargon!

n	sum of the natural numbers
2	$1 + 2 = 3$
3	$1 + 2 + 3 = 6$
4	$1 + 2 + 3 + 4 = 10$

and so on.

So the problem is to enter any number and get out the sum of the integers from 1 up to and including that number.

EXERCISE 7.2*

If you are tiring of numbers then you can try a PROLOG classic of recursion and that is the 'ancestor' problem. We devised a rule for parent-of at the end of Chapter 2, and went on to think about grand-parents. You can define **ancestor-of** in terms of **ancestor-of** or **parent-of** as the limiting case. Extend the ROYAL3 data-base to test your **ancestor-of** rule.

7.4   Theatre seats

Up to this point our programs have consisted of single relationships. These have begun to get quite complicated in themselves, with up to six or even more sentences in each rule. The tendency in micro-PROLOG is to have fairly short rules, with a program being a collection of such rules. In this example we make a first attempt at writing such a program.

The aim of the program is to let a customer place an order and receive a bill for some theatre seats. It is modelling a fragment of a real-life situation, acting like an interactive till if you like, and so in a small way it is our first **simulaton** program in micro-PROLOG. We will follow through our four rules of problem solving yet again, and try to illustrate the top-down method of programming which I mentioned earlier.

If you think about the overall effect of the program, it will be to produce a bill for the customer. To do this the program must somehow calculate the total cost of the customer's order, and then display this amount on the screen or print it on paper. So the top rule of our program would look something like:

bill the customer by calculating the total cost and
        by printing it out

This is all very well but it leaves a lot of questions un-answered. This feeling of 'But — what about?' is the essence of top-down programming; you are working from the most general statement to the most specific, and so until you get to the final rule there will always be questions left un-answered.

But — what about the total cost, how can you calculate it until you know what the customer has ordered — and so on? Let's take it step by step. To calculate the total cost you need to know and deal with two items of data: how many seats the customer wants, and the price of these seats. To make it seem a little more realistic, but not add too much detail which would confuse the program, I have assumed that there would be just two types of seat in the theatre — stalls and circle. So the total cost may be broken down into a rule involving the costs for these two types of seat:

total cost = stalls cost + circle cost

In the same way you can write the stalls cost in a rule something like

stalls cost = number of seats requested × cost of a seat

The phrase 'seats requested' will introduce a new technique in PROLOG, because it will involve accepting into a program data from the keyboard. But we are currently involved in analysing the problem in general terms, and not at stage 2 of actually forming a plan. So I will leave it for now in the form:

stalls cost by asking for number of seats to be input and
                receiving this data and
                calculating number of seats × cost of a seat

There will have to be a similar rule for the circle cost. Finally at the bottom of this top down program we will store the price of stalls and circle seats as data sentences.

So the general collection of rules which forms the program is:

1   bill the customer with the total cost
2   derive the total cost from the stalls and circle costs
3   derive the stalls cost
4   derive the circle cost

You can see the top-down structure where each rule calls others lower down in the program.

You now understand the problem, and are more than ready to enter stage 2 of the problem solving process, and write some micro-PROLOG rules. Most of the rules are very straight-forward and so I will concentrate on the interactive rules 3 and 4, starting with a small digression into the **R** command.

7.4.1   THE **R** COMMAND

R stands for Read, and like **P** and **PP**, forms a sentence which is always true. It is a compulsory unary relationship and so forms a procedure which must be carried out for the program to continue. You will see what is happening from the following snippet of program. I entered the following rule as:

```
&add(number-in-stalls X if
1P(How many stalls seats?) and
1R(X))
&.
```

Here **R(X)** means 'read in a value from the keyboard, and as far as this rule is concerned, take what is entered as the value of the variable **X**'. It is the only fact in the machine so:

```
&list all
number-in-stalls X if
        P (How many stalls seats ?) and
        X R
&which(x:number-in-stalls x)
How many stalls seats ?13
13
No (more) answers
&.
```

There are some details which are worth noting. Some spaces have occurred between **P** and first bracket, and the second **s** of **seats** and the **?** Yes, they are details but they are not printing errors. The next point to note is that **R(X)** as entered has become **X R** in the listing — this is just micro-PROLOG re-arranging the unary relationship in its standard form.

After the **which** query, the **P**(message) sentence prints out the message, and the screen looks like **How many stalls seats ?.** . The message is followed by the dot-prompt, and the system waits at that point until the user enters something at the keyboard. In this case I entered **13**, and the **1** of **13** over-wrote the dot-prompt. The system will not continue until an input is made, so that is why I said it is a procedure which must be carried out for the program to proceed.

You are now in the position to embellish your programs with zaney comments, if that is the style of interaction you favour. Note the tone of waspish disapproval creeping in here! You may like programs which welcome you in the following way:

```
&list welcome
user welcome if
        P (Hello ! What is your name?) and
        X R and
        PP (Hi X welcome to my program!)
&.
```

However, there is something new here. The rule has been defined by a unary sentence **user welcome**, it contains no variables, so how do you query it? You cannot use a **which** because there are no variables, so the only technique you have left is **is**:

```
&is(user welcome)
Hello ! What is your name ?Fred
Hi Fred welcome to my program !
YES
&.
```

So, it does work. Note how the value for **X** entered at the keyboard is substituted into the **PP**(message) sentence, and that that value is not a number this time, but a name, a string of characters. This use of the **is** query mode is rather artificial here, and leaves us with the inappropriate **YES** at the end. All quite logical but rather strange!

One very appropriate feature of micro-PROLOG is that if a rule is defined by a unary sentence without variables, then if the sentence is reversed it changes into a command to activate the rule. In this case if **user welcome** is reversed to give **welcome user**, its imperative nature does appropriately become a command:

```
&welcome user
Hello ! What is your name ?Hetty
Hi Hetty welcome to my program !
&.
```

As you see we have also lost the strange **YES** off the end of the run as well.

7.4.2   BACK TO THEATRE SEATS

We are in stage 2 attempting to turn the solutions we have written out in English sentences into a plan in micro-PROLOG. Having planned the solution top-down we will now code it into micro-PROLOG from the bottom up. So you can start with rules 3 and 4 above.

> stalls cost by asking for number of seats to be input and
>> receiving this data and
>> calculating number of seats × cost of a seat

In micro-PROLOG this will look like:

> **stalls cost-is X if**
>> **P (How many stalls seats ?) and**
>> **Y R and**
>> **stalls price-is Z and**
>> **TIMES(Y Z X)**

The number entered from the keyboard goes into variable **Y**, and is then multiplied by **Z**, the price of a stalls seat which is stored as a sentence in the data-base, and so the stalls cost $X = Z \times Y$. If you replace **stalls** with **circle** in the above rule you will have a rule to find the cost of the circle seats.

The remainder of the program is straight-forward, and you can identify rules 1–4 quite clearly. Top to bottom it is given in Listing 7.3.

> **&list all**
> **customer bill if**
>> **total cost-is X and**
>> **PP and**
>> **PP (The total cost is X) and**
>> **PP and**
>> **PP (Enjoy the show .)**
> **total cost-is X if**
>> **stalls cost-is Y and**
>> **circle cost-is Z and**
>> **SUM(Y Z X)**
> **stalls cost-is X if**
>> **P (How many stalls seats ?) and**
>> **Y R and**
>> **stalls price-is Z and**
>> **TIMES(Y Z X)**
> **circle cost-is x if**
>> **P (how many circle seats ?) and**
>> **Y R and**
>> **circle price-is Z and**
>> **TIMES(Y Z X)**
> **stalls price-is 8.5**
> **circle price-is 14.5**
> **&.**

Listing 7.3

PP on its own just prints a blank line, and is used to display the output just a little more attractively. The command **bill customer** will start the execution of the program:

> **&bill customer**
> **How many stalls seats ?3**
> **How many circle seats ?4**
>
> **The total cost is 83.5**
>
> **Enjoy the show .**
> **&.**

Stage 3 'carry out the plan' has been completed in the 'run' of the program. It has done its job accurately enough. It is not entirely satisfactory because the average customer will only wish to purchase seats in one part of the theatre, and the program makes you provide answers to both stalls and circle. If you do not want tickets for one type of seat, then you have to answer 0 to that particular question from the machine:

&bill customer
How many stalls seats ?0
How many circle seats ?4

The total cost is 58

Enjoy the show .
&.

Entering the final stage of reviewing the program, it is obvious that its scope is limited; but it was designed with this in mind, to provide a simple example of what is meant by the top-down technique. There are many improvements which would have to be made to make it really useful. It would have to deal with a much wider variety of types of seat, and with different prices for evening and matinee performances. The way it works at the moment is that it only processes one request for tickets, and then the program has to be re-run. So another improvement would be to build in a repetitive feature.

In real life you would want the program to have a data-base of the seating arrangements of the theatre, so that it could allocate seats as well as provide a bill. A very serious defect of the program itself is that it does not check the information that is entered at the keyboard. In replying to the question **How many stalls seats?** the customer could reply with ridiculously large or small numbers, or fractions or negative numbers, and still have the bill calculated for that number of seats. So there is a long way to go to make this program into a useful tool.

7.5   Synonyms

We will now put together a solution to a different type of problem, and find that the overall program looks quite similar in general outline to theatre seats. It models another interactive situation where the user is thought to be someone who is writing in English and who wants ready access to synonyms, words which have similar meanings — author, journalist, business person, english teacher or possibly just someone with an interest in crossword puzzles. Yes, I know that there are some very good dictionaries or guides to synonyms available in book form, but I'm just projecting into the future when word-processors may have lists of synonyms as well as dictionaries to help you spell correctly.

The problem then is for the user to enter a word at the keyboard and for the machine to display a group of synonyms for that word, if they are available. I will not describe my solution to this problem in quite such simplistic detail as the last. You can see the overall structure as input-process-output:

input a word → find synonyms → output the synonyms

So, the first stage of the top-down process may look like

> synonym search if
> > user enters word
> > machine finds synonyms
> > display synonyms
> > repeat the process

Now it begins to look familiar and reasonably straight-forward, but there are a few pot-holes which we have to avoid or cope with in some way. The most important thing about these top-down procedures written in the form of one rule, is that all of the stages of the rule have to be true for the program to work. There must be no loose ends left along the way or the program will 'hang-up'. This means that a phrase such as 'finds synonyms' has got to cope with the case when no synonyms are found, and pass some sort of data on to the 'display' stage, so that that stage will be true as well.

This consideration affects how the collections of synonyms is stored in the program. The number of synonyms that words have is, of course, variable, and your first thoughts about the solution may be to allow this, and to store them in the form of lists, and then to use **item-in** from the last chapter. This copes with the case when the word entered is in the synonym lists, but it does raise some difficult problems when the word is not there. When the **back-tracking** process occurs in the recursion, it leaves a trail of unsolved problems which can cause the program to fail unless controlled very carefully, and this involves technical matters which we have not yet encountered.

As it is the overall program which I am interested in, I will pose a simpler version of the problem, where the synonyms are collected in sets of only four words, and stored in lists of this fixed length. So the basic data for the program will be stored in sentences like:

> **(forget neglect omit overlook) are-synonyms**

This about completes the stage 1 part of solving the problem; you should by now have a clear picture of what the problem is. So I will move on to stage 2 to devise a plan, or program to solve the problem.

The 'user enters word' and 'display synonyms' are fairly straight-forward sequences involving **P**, **PP** and **R**, similar to the previous program. I have used **PP( )** liberally to space out the comments, inputs and outputs, because if not the screen does get quite cluttered. You will be able to see what is happening from the listing of the program. Remember **PP( )** appears as just **PP** in the listing, and **R(X)** as **X R**.

Let us concentrate on finding the synonyms. The word entered at the keyboard may be at any one of the four positions in the list. If the word is at the first position it will be found by a statement of the form:

> **X found-in (X x1 x2 x3) if (X x1 x2 x3) are-synonyms**

and if it is at the second position:

> **X found-in (x1 X x2 x3) if (x1 X x2 x3) are-synonyms**

and so on with two more rules for the third and fourth places.

We can say that the word entered has synonyms if the word is found in the **are-synonyms** lists. A rule of the following form will carry out this task:

> **X has-synonyms Y if X found-in Y**

But the word may not be found in any of the lists, and we need a positive statement to cover this instance, so I say that the synonyms form an empty list in this case:

X has-synonyms ( ) if not X found-in Y

You will be able to read through the final program (Listing 7.4) now and get the whole picture.

```
&list all
syns search if
        X word-entered and
        X has-syns Y and
        Y is-shown and
        syns search
X word-entered if
        PP and
        P (What is your word ?) and
        X R
X has-syns Y if
        X found-in Y
X has-syns ( ) if
        not X found-in Y
X found-in (Y Z x X) if
        (Y Z x X) are-syns
X found-in (Y Z X x) if
        (Y Z X x) are-syns
X found-in (Y X Z x) if
        (Y X Z x) are-syns
X found-in (X Y Z x) if
        (X Y Z x) are-syns
( ) is-shown if
        PP and
        PP (I cannot find your word !) and
        PP
X is-shown if
        PP and
        PP (Here is a list of synonyms) and
        PP (which includes your word) and
        PP and
        X PP and
        PP
(component constituent element ingredient) are-syns
(effect cause produce realize) are-syns
(forget neglect omit overlook) are-syns
(include comprise contain involve) are-syns
(bounce cannon deflect ricochet) are-syns
(class caste estate order) are-syns
&.
```

Listing 7.4

I have shortened **synonyms** to **syns** in the program statements to lighten the typing load for me, and you perhaps! Note that the first rule **syns search** ends with **syns search**, which makes the whole program recursive, and so it will go on and on requesting you to enter a word. The only way you can stop it, at this stage in our knowledge, is to press the Escape key to abort the run. If you have typed in the program then the first thing to do is to save it, because you do not want to waste all that hard work. You will see how it behaves from the run, which we activate as before by turning **syns search** into the command **search syns**.

&search syns

What is your word ?element

**Here is a list of synonyms
which includes your word**

(component constituent element ingredient)

What is your word ?omitt

I cannot find that word !

What is your word ?

The program will just go on requesting more and more words until you abort it, or until it runs out of memory space because PROLOG keeps track of all its solutions and slowly but surely uses up its memory.

The program seems to do what it was intended to do, so stage 3 has been satisfied. There is much to say in stage 4, but we must remember that it is more of an exercise than a realistic problem. The data-bank would have to be huge to be really useful. The groups of four synonyms are not very realistic. You would have to try and cope with alternative spelling e.g. 'realise' or 'realize', for plurals etc. You would have to stop it using memory at such a rate, and so on.

EXERCISE 7.3*

Modify the Synonyms program above to act as Translator, by forming a data-base of English and foreign words, and when an English word is input from the keyboard its foreign equivalent is shown on the screen.

Such a program could then be easily modified to make a Vocabulary Testing program. Display an English word on the screen, ask for the user to input its French equivalent, and reply whether the user's answer is correct or not. It could also be modified to cope with the transposition of melodies or chords from one key to another.

EXERCISE 7.4

Design a Multiple Choice program. For example the machine offers:

Keyword . . . Acumen
1 . . . Accuracy
2 . . . Shrewdness
3 . . . Force
4 . . . Obtuseness

Select the word or phrase whose meaning is closest to that of the keyword . . .

after which the user has to supply 1, 2, 3 or 4 as his/her answer. The machine then replies with a suitable message. You know the sort of questioning, and can change the subject matter from the word test above, to something which interests you.

8
List programs for the classroom

8.1 Introduction

This is the longest chapter of the book with possibly the greatest variety of elementary programs. Many of the programs are extensions of ideas which were introduced earlier, and a few prepare you for the larger programs of Chapter 9. They all involve the processing of lists in some form or other. Although the theme of the examples is largely determined by activities which would appear in the classroom more frequently than elsewhere, the techniques involved have much wider application, and for these and other reasons, I balked at entitling the chapter Educational Programs.

I start by concocting a Statistics program which calculates the maximum and minimum values, the range and mean of the values in a list. The chapter proceeds to look at how sets may be represented by lists, and develops programs for the intersection and union of sets. Finally I return to the powerful **append-to** program which was introduced in Chapter 6, and use it to look at deletion, segmentation and sentence division, the generation of permutations of the items in a list, and finally to ordering and a glimpse at sorting the items. Two new operators emerge, **isall** and **forall**, and recursion appears in almost every program.

```
&list all
X greater-of (X X)
X greater-of (X Y) if
     Y LESS X
X greater-of (Y X) if
     Y LESS X
&which(x:x greater-of (7 2))
7
No (more) answers
&which(x:x greater-of (7 22))
22
No (more) answers
&which(x:x greater-of (7 7))
7
No (more) answers
&.
```

Listing 8.1

8.2　Maximum and minimum values

In Chapter 6 we wrote programs to identify the individual items in a list, to add up their values if the items were numbers, to count them, and thus on to calculating the arithmetic mean (or average) of the values in the list. The next stage in the statistical process would be to look at the range of values in the list, by finding the maximum value and the minimum value, and, from their difference, the range of values, and that is where we are going to start in this first part of the chapter.

The way that you find the maximum value in a list is to compare neighbouring pairs of values along its length. So, let's start by looking at the rule for finding the greater of a pair of values. By the word 'pair' I mean a list with just two items in it. The relationship **greater-of** links an individual value to the pair of values in the list. I think that you will find the rule and its test runs shown in Listing 8.1 self-explanatory.

The three sentences of the rule cater for the cases where the two numbers are equal, where the first of the pair is the greater, and the third rule is for where the second of the pair is the greater. The three test cases cover these three possibilities. I have chosen to start by looking at numbers, but you may well ask whether the rule will also apply to strings of characters. So, let's try it!

```
&which(x:x greater-of (a b))
b
No (more) answers
&which(x:x greater-of (cain abel)
cain
No (more) answers
&which(x:x greater-of (hit hat))
hit
No (more) answers
&which(x:x greater-of (john johns))
johns
No (more) answers
&.
```

You will recall what I said earlier about the numerical representation of individual characters in the ASCII code, so you will not be at all surprised that **b** was selected as the greater of **(a b)**, and that **cain** was selected as the greater of **(cain abel)**, because on the ASCII code the number representing a is 97, b is 98 and c is 99. I have also included the slightly less clear cut case **(hit hat)**, where the character strings differ only in the second character **i** and **a** respectively, but **'hit'** was chosen as the greater of the pair. In similar vein I chose **(john johns)** which differ only in the fifth character. You should be convinced that character strings are compared on the basis of the combined numerical values of the individual characters of the string, as if the values are added together to give an overall value for the whole string. The net effect anyway, is that words or names are sorted into alphabetical order in the sense in which the term is usually used, with the end of the alphabet having the higher numerical values on the ASCII coding scheme.

EXERCISE 8.1

(a)　Write a PROLOG rule to find the **smaller-of** a pair of values in a list.

(b)　If you feel that you would benefit from using the interactive techniques which

I introduced in the last chapter, then you could re-write **greater-of** in an interactive manner. Put a prompt on the screen to input the pair as a list, and output the greater value with an appropriate message. Allow for the case where the pair are equal.

To find the maximum value of a whole list rather than just a pair of values, you have to treat the list as a succession of pairs of values. You take the first pair of a list, find the greater value of that pair, and then replace the list with this single larger value and the tail of the original list, and then repeat the operation. The idea of a succession of pairs, and a series of lists which are getting shorter and shorter as you continue along the list, leads naturally to a recursive rule. Look at the following rule:

> **(X) max-is X**
> **(X Y│Z) max-is x if**
>   **y greater-of (X Y) and**
>   **(y│Z) max-is x**

The first sentence is the non-recursive part of the rule, and simply says that the maximum value in a one item list is the single value itself. The second sentence sees the list split into the pair of values **(X Y)** and a tail **Z: (X Y│Z)**. It goes on to claim that **x** will be the maximum value in that list if **y** is the greater of the pair **(X Y)**, and **x** is the maximum value of the remaining list **(y│Z)**. Thus control is sent back to the first sentence for a re-test, and on to sentence two again if it does not apply, and so recursion occurs.

To really see what is happening here you feel you ought to be able to load in SIMTRAC and trace the solution path of this rule. That is all very well if you have enough memory space to take the SIMTRAC module and hold the solutions to this program. With the BBC micro I have found that you only have room to attempt to trace the solutions of a list with two or three items in it, and even then it runs out of memory space before the trace is complete. I hope by the time this book is published, this situation will have been rectified. In the meantime I will resort to my previous home-brew method of building in a primitive trace procedure using print commands (see Listing 8.2). It will give a fairly good guide to the processes which are involved:

In trying to solve **max-is** a number of intermediary solutions to **greater-of** must be found. These are shown in the five print-outs for either **greater-of2** or **greater-of3**. Notice how each pair of values in these print-outs is formed: **8** is the greater of **8** and **1**, so **8** is passed on down the list and compared with **2**, and then passed on and compared with **9**, whereupon **9** becomes the current maximum and so on down the list. The greater of each pair is always shown first because the way that **greater-of** is written makes **X** the greater of each pair. When this intermediate process is complete **9** is the sole member of the list and so this value is output by the first sentence of **max-is** as shown by **max1**. But this is only one solution state

Table 8.1

X	Y	Z the tail	x	y
9	4	()	9	9
9	5	(4)	9	9
8	9	(5 4)	9	9
8	2	(9 5 4)	9	8
1	8	(2 9 5 4)	9	8

```
&list all
(X) max-is X if
     max1 PP X
(X Y | Z)max-is x if
     y greater-of (X Y) and
     (y | Z) max-is x and
     PP (max2 X Y Z x y)
X greater-of (X X) if
     greater-of1 PP X
X greater-of (X Y) if
     Y LESS X and
     PP (greater-of2 X Y )
X greater-of (Y X) if
     Y LESS X and
     PP (greater-of3 X Y)
&.which(x:(1 8 2 9 5 4) max-is x)
greater-of3 8 1
greater-of2 8 2
greater-of3 9 8
greater-of2 9 5
greater-of2 9 4
max1 9
max2 9 4 ( ) 9 9
max2 9 5 (4) 9 9
max2 8 9 (5 4) 9 9
max2 8 2 (9 5 4) 9 8
max2 1 8 (2 9 5 4) 9 8
9
No (more) answers
&.
```

Listing 8.2

to the problem — the interpreter then continues to output all of the other solution states which are possible. If you set these values out as in Table 8.1 you get a clearer picture of what is going on.

If you are still a little hazy about how the list was sectioned in the first instance you can read the table upwards from bottom to top, and looking at the first three columns only shows how the list is cut up into leading pair and tail, until the tail is ( ) and the partitioning process stops. As you can see the actual solution process is this sectioning process in reverse, after the maximum value has already been found, hence the values in the **x** and **y** columns of the table.

EXERCISE 8.2

(a)   Write a **min-is** program to find the minimum value in a list, using the **smaller-of** rule which you devised in Exercise 8.1.

(b)   Write a **range-is** program to find the range of values in a list. You will recall that the range = max. value − min. value.

8.3   Statistics program

We are now in a position to stitch together all of the little statistical routines which we have collected through the course of the book into one statistics program. The function of the program will be to let you enter a list of numbers at the keyboard and then display on the screen the total number of items in the list, their sum, the arithmetic mean, the maximum and minimum values and the range. If you feel that you are in a position to do this for yourself, then you should treat this task as an exercise before looking at my solution in detail.

You can see that in outline the program will have the following form:

statistics calculation
enter the list
calculate the mean and print out the value
calculate the range and printout the value

In terms of the program routines which we have already written we can show how they are used in the following way:

mean-is	→	**total-is**	→	**count-is**
range-is	→	**max-is**	→	**greater-of**
	→	**min-is**	→	**smaller-of**

I'm sure that there is no need for further explanation, and that you will find Listing 8.3 is quite straight forward:

```
&list all
stats calc if
      X enter-list and
      X mean-is Y and
      P (The mean is :) and
      Y PP and
      X range-is Z and
      P (The range is :) and
      Z PP
X enter-list if
      PP (Enter list of numbers below) and
      X R
X mean-is Y if
      X total-is Z and
      P (The total is :) and
      Z PP and
      X count-is x and
      P (The number of values is :) and
      x PP and
      TIMES (Y X Z)
X range-is Y if
      X max-is Z and
      P (The maximum value is :) and
      Z PP and
      X min-is x and
      P (The minimum value is :) and
      x PP and
      SUM (Y X Z)
( ) total-is 0
(X|Y) total-is Z if
      Y total-is x and
```

```
                    SUM (x X Z)
             ( ) count-is 0
             (X | Y) count-is Z if
                    Y count-is x and
                    SUM(x 1 Z)
             (X) max-is X
             (X Y | Z) max-is x if
                    y greater-of (X Y) and
                    (y | Z) max-is x
             X greater-of (X X)
             X greater-of (X Y) if
                    Y LESS X
             X greater-of (Y X) if
                    Y LESS X
             (X) min-is X
             (X Y | Z) min-is x if
                    y smaller-of (X Y) and
                    (y | Z) min-is x
             X smaller-of (X X)
             X smaller-of (X Y) if
                       X LESS Y
             X LESS Y
             X smaller-of (Y X) if
             X LESS Y
             &calc stats
             Enter list of numbers below
             (−11 8 13 −2 5 9 −4 12 15 −6)
             The total is :39
             The number of values is :10
             The mean is :3.9
             The maximum value is :15
             The minimum value is :−11
             The range is :26
             &.
```

Listing 8.3

The program started with the rule **stats calc if** etc., and you will recall from the last chapter how this is turned into a command **calc stats** to start the execution of the program, as you can see from the trial run above.

8.4   The **isall** operator

The more programming you do in micro-PROLOG, the more you appreciate the importance of lists. It is possible to obtain the answers to an elementary query in the form of a list. To do this we use the **isall** operator. Glance back at the ROYAL2 file in Chapter 1, and imagine that you have that file in the memory of the machine, and then pose the following queries:

```
        &which(x:x isall(y:y male))
        (Philip Charles William Henry)
        No (more) answers
        &which(x:x isall(y:y female))
        (Elizabeth Anne Diana)
        No (more) answers
        &.
```

You see that the answer to this type of query gives the data in the form of a list. You can ask more complicated questions using the **isall** operator:

&**which(x:x isall(y:(either y mother-of z or y father-of z)))**
(Elizabeth Elizabeth Diana Diana Philip Philip Charles Charles)
No (more) answers
&**.**

You will have noticed how micro-PROLOG in its pedantic thoroughness has found all of the instances of **mother-of** and **father-of**, and so has generated the repeats in the list.

You can read the **(x:x isall**(. . .(conditions). . .)**)** as '**x** is a list of all the answers which obey the . . .(conditions). . .' so **isall** can be seen as a short-hand version of 'is a list of all'. More formally if you see the expression involving **isall** as having the form:

   (Answer pattern **isall (**. . .conditions. . .**))**

then the result is a list of all of the answer patterns which obey the given conditions.

The **isall** operator is one of the most powerful tools in micro-PROLOG's armoury of list processing functions. I have chosen to illustrate the use of **isall** by looking at some elementary ideas about sets. A word of warning before I do, however, and that is to say that some versions of micro-PROLOG, when evaluating the **isall** operator, output the list in the reverse order to that in which the facts are stored in the data-base. The Acornsoft version of the language does output the lists in the order in which they are found in the data-base, as shown in the runs of the queries above. If you are using other versions of micro-PROLOG, take care to check out this point, because it can make some subtle changes to the way in which the programs work.

EXERCISE 8.3*

Write a program to find the squares of numbers in a list, and the sum of these squares.

8.5   Sets

The ideas of sets (see Fig. 8.1(a)–(d)) embody a lot of common sense, and are fundamental to mathematical thought and to the origins of micro-PROLOG itself. We have already met some of the basic ideas in Chapter 5 when we looked at the logic operators 'and' and 'not', but we were then concerned only with lists of fixed length and had not met open lists and the **item-in** type of routine. Sets are seldom going to be of a pre-determined size, and so the looser approach of open lists is necessary. As you will have realised by now I am going to represent the members of a set by items in a list, and so here the ideas of sets and lists are inextricably linked together, as are sets and logic. The two basic ideas in sets are **union** and **intersection**.

8.5.1   THE UNION OF SETS

The union of two sets, is the set which consists of all of the members of both sets. So if set Y has the elements a b c and d, which I will show as Y = (a b c d), and set Z

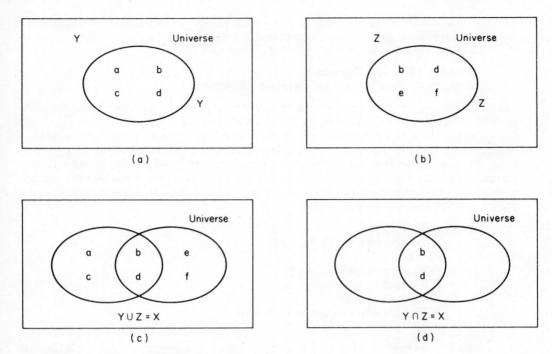

Fig. 8.1 Sets—the Universe is all students in a class
    (a)   Y shows all students studying Physics
    (b)   Z shows all students studying Chemistry
    (c)   The Union (Y ∪ Z = X) i.e. all students studying *either* Physics *or* Chemistry
    (d)   The Intersection (Y ∩ Z = X) i.e. all students studying *both* Physics *and* Chemistry

has elements b d e and f, or Z = (b d e f) then

    the union X of Y and Z is the set a b c d e f

or

    X = Y union Z = (a b c d e f)

You will have noted that if we look at these sets as lists then the union of two sets is different from the list we would get by appending the list Z to the list Y, which would be (a b c d b d e f), that is, the appended list would include the two elements b and d repeated. Fig. 8.1(c) shows the usual textbook picture of the union of two sets. In practical terms if Y represented the names of all those students who were studying Physics in a college, and Z all those who were studying Chemistry, then X, the union set, would represent all those who were studying either Physics or Chemistry — the union list would not include twice the names of those who were studying both subjects. From the above discussion we are in a position to suggest a two-fold rule for union which is translatable into micro-PROLOG:

    X is a member of the union of Y and Z if X is a member of Y

and the second instance

    X is a member of the union of Y and Z if X is a member of Z and
    not also a member of Y

The routine which looked at each item in a list which we developed in Chapter 6, and called **item-in**, can be used to pick out the members of a list. So, we can turn the two sentences above into micro-PROLOG sentences:

> **X union (Y Z) if X item-in Y**
> **X union (Y Z) if X item-in Z and not(X item-in Y)**

I will not list and run this snippet of a program now but you may rest assured that it does do the job, when it is called by the **union2** routine listed below.

One other important piece of information which you would wish to know when you operate on sets, is how many members there are in the resulting sets. In this case, how many elements are there in the union of the two sets? The routine **union2**, so called because it describes the union of two sets, involves the **union** routine, and the **count-is** routine from Chapter 6 as well as some print statements which output the required data:

> **X union2 (Y Z) if**
> **X isall(x:x union (Y Z)) and**
> **PP and**
> **P(The union set is:) and**
> **X PP and**
> **X count-is y and**
> **P(The number in the set is:) and**
> **y PP**

So, **union2** finds the union of sets **Y** and **Z** and puts the items into the list **X**, prints out this list, then counts the number of items in this list and prints out that result.

8.5.2   THE INTERSECTION OF SETS

The intersection of two sets will be a set whose members are common to both of the original sets. In the example sets I took above viz Y = (a b c d) and Z = (b d e f) then the intersection set X = (b d), that is, only those two members which occur in both Y and Z (Fig. 8.1(d)). Similarly in the example of the two sets of students, those who are studying Physics, and the other the set of those who are studying Chemistry, the intersection would be only those students who are studying both Physics and Chemistry. This situation is directly analogous to the logic function 'and', and so you will readily see that it is achieved by the following program sentence:

> **X isall(x:x item-in Y and x item-in Z)**

EXAMPLE 8.1   PROGRAM FOR TWO SETS

I suggest a program which is controlled by the first routine of the SETS program, the top or controlling routine of the 'top-down' program of routines.

> **sets two if**
> **enter-sets (X Y) and**
> **Z intersection2 (X Y) and**
> **x union2 (X Y)**

The result of **intersection2** and **union2** is to form the intersection and union of the two sets, and to find the number in each set, and each routine should output these results, as outlined in the **union2** routine above. You need to write an **enter-sets** routine, and to remember that you will have to include the **union** sentences above,

```
&list all
sets two if
      X enter-sets Y and
      Z intersection2 (X Y) and
      x union2 (X Y)
X enter-sets Y if
       PP and
       PP(Enter first set as a list) and
       X R and
       PP(Enter second set as a list) and
       Y R
X intersection2 (Y Z) if
      X isall(x:x item-in Y and x item-in Z) and
      PP and
      P(The intersection set is:) and
      X PP and
      X count-is y and
      P(The number in the set is:) and
      y PP
X union2 (Y Z) if
      X isall(x:x union (Y Z)) and
      PP and
      P(The union set is:) and
      X PP and
      X count-is y and
      P(The number in the set is:) and
      y PP
X union (Y Z) if
      X item-in Y
X union (Y Z) if
      X item-in Z and
      not(X item-in Y)
X item-in (X|Y)
X item-in (Y|Z) if
      X item-in Z
( ) count-is 0
(X|Y) count-is Z if
       Y count-is x and
       SUM(x 1 Z)
&two sets

Enter first set as a list
(a b c d)
Enter second set as a list
(b d e f)

The intersection set is:(b d)
The number in the set is:2

The union set is:(a b c d e f)
The number in the set is:6
&.
```

Listing 8.4   SETS program and run

and the **item-in** and **count-is** routines from Chapter 6. So, the exercise is really one of stitching together all of these routines under the control of the 'top' routine given above. Try to write the whole of the program for yourself before looking at my solution shown in Listing 8.4.

A more life-like example, rather than just abstract letters, could be taken from the Animals data of earlier chapters. Also these sets are not of equal length, as were the two sets used to test the program above. The first set will be those animals with legs, and the second those with fur.

> **&two sets**
>
> **Enter the first set as a list**
> **(birds frogs crocodile lizards tigers humans horses)**
> **Enter the second set as a list**
> **(tigers humans horses dolphins whales)**
>
> **The intersection set is:(tigers humans horses)**
> **The number in the set is:3**
>
> **The union set is:(birds frogs crocodiles lizards tigers humans**
> **horses dolphins whales)**
> **The number in the set is:9**
> **&.**

EXERCISE 8.4

Once again this is a suggestion rather than an Exercise with a model answer. If you are interested in the elementary ideas of sets then you will readily see how the above program can be extended to cope with the typical school problem of the union and intersection of three sets, and the sub-sets generated, and of the possibility of including the formulae giving the numbers of members in the various sub-sets.

8.6   Functions which use **append-to**

At the end of Chapter 6 I had just introduced you to the **append-to** program, and left you with some exercises which I hope caused you to think a little more deeply about this function. If I were asked to name the most important single program routine in elementary micro-PROLOG I would name **append-to**. So, I make no apologies for having introduced it earlier, and for starting this section by reviewing its use:

> **&list all**
> **(( ) X) append-to X**
> **((X|Y) Z) append-to (X|x) if**
> **   (Y Z) append-to x**
> **&which(x:((a b c) (d e f)) append-to x)**
> **(a b c d e f)**
> **No (more) answers**
> **&.**

I prefer this definition of **append-to** to that of **append(X Y Z)** which I left for you as an exercise, and which is often preferred by other authors — mainly because it reads more naturally: 'lists **X** and **Y** append to **Z**'. It can be used to build up lists, as the program run shows, but like so many other functions in micro-PROLOG it can be used backwards. The following runs show how it can be used backwards to break down lists into their component parts:

    &which(x y:(x y) append-to (a b c d e))
    ( ) (a b c d e)
    (a) (b c d e)
    (a b) (c d e)
    (a b c) (d e)
    (a b c d) (e)
    (a b c d e) ( )
    No (more) answers
    &.

With typical micro-PROLOG thoroughness this query shows all of the different ways in which sub-lists may be appended to give **(a b c d e)**. Or, if you wish to read it backwards, all of the ways the list can be broken down into sub-lists. To revise your ideas about list notation, what will be the differences between the solutions to the above query, and those to the following one?

    &which((x | X) (y|Y):(x|X) (y|Y)) append-to (a b c d e))

Come on, play the game and do not look at the solutions until you have thought it through for yourself!

    (a) (b c d e)
    (a b) (c d e)
    (a b c) (d e)
    (a b c d) (e)
    No (more) answers
    &.

Yes, the notation **(x|X)** implies an element **x**, followed by a list **X**, but **( )** is an empty list and not an element, so the solutions to the second query will not include the first and last solutions to the first query which involved **( )**.
  You can use these ideas to split a list at a given element **b** in this case:

    &which(x (b|Y):(x (b|Y)) append-to (a b c d b f))
    (a) (b c d b f)
    (a b c d) (b f)
    No (more) answers
    &.

or ask the same question in a slightly more general way:

    &which(x (y|Y):(x (y|Y)) append-to
    (a b c d b f) and y EQ b)

This gives the same answer — but so what? Well, if I pose the question of slightly more meaningful data, you will begin to see the drift.

```
&which(x (y|Y):(x (y|Y)) append-to
l(a the c d the e f) and y EQ the)
(a) (the c d the e f)
(a the c d) (the e f)
No (more) answers
&.
```

```
&which(x (y|Y):(x (y|Y)) append-to
l(a the c a d the e f) and
l(either y EQ a or y EQ the))
( ) (a the c a d the e f)
(a) (the c a d the e f)
(a the c) (a d the e f)
(a the c a d) (the e f)
No (more) answers
&.
```

The above programs divided up the lists into sub-lists, starting at **a** or **the**, so if we think of a sentence as just a list of words then we could use these ideas to split the sentences into their constituent parts — in this example if the parts start with **a** or **the** then they could be noun clauses:

```
&which(x (y|Y):(x (y|Y)) append-to
l(the sun shone on a deep blue sea) and
l(either y EQ a or y EQ the))
( ) (The sun shone on a deep blue sea)
(the sun shone on) (a deep blue sea)
No (more) answers
&which(x (y|Y):(x (y|Y)) append-to
l(the walrus and the carpenter walked on a mile or so) and
l(either y EQ a or y EQ the))
( ) (The walrus and the carpenter walked on a mile or so)
(the walrus and) (the carpenter walked on a mile or so)
(the walrus and the carpenter walked on) (a mile or so)
No (more) answers
&.
```

This could be the start of efforts to write a program to parse sentences. Research into natural languages has always interested researchers in Artificial Intelligence, and here we can see a possible albeit very elementary starting point. We will do some exercises which will extend these ideas.

EXERCISE 8.5*

(a)   Write a routine which will delete an item from a list. **(X Y) deletes-to Z** does not have the same natural sense as **appends-to**, so I suggest you choose **del (X Y Z)** meaning 'deleting **X** from **Y** gives you **Z**'. Use **del** rather than 'delete' because this word is protected because of its wider and potentially drastic usage in the language.

EXAMPLE 8.2

(b) I have written a program which splits a list into its front and back segments using **appends-to**, and the effect of these two routines is shown below:

> **&which(x:x frontsegof (a b c d))**
> **(a)**
> **(a b)**
> **(a b c)**
> **(a b c d)**
> **No (more) answers**
> **&which(x:x backsegof (a b c d))**
> **(a b c d)**
> **(b c d)**
> **(c d)**
> **(d)**
> **No (more) answers**
> **&.**

Write the routines for **frontsegof** and **backsegof** and then combine them into a general rule **segof** which separates out all of the possible segments of a list.

Segment solution

My solution is shown in Listing 8.5.

> **&list all**
> **X segof Y if**
> **Z backsegof Y and**
> **X frontsegof Z**
> **(X|Y) frontsegof Z if**
> **((X|Y) x) append-to Z**
> **(X|Y) backsegof Z if**
> **(x (X|Y)) append-to Z**
> **(( ) X) append-to X**
> **((X|Y) Z) append-to (X|x) if**
> **(Y Z) append-to x**
> **( ) count-is 0**
> **(X|Y) count-is Z if**
> **Y count-is x and**
> **SUM(x 1 Z)**
> **&which(x:x segof (a b c d))**
> **(a)**
> **(a b)**
> **(a b c)**
> **(a b c d)**
> **(b)**
> **(b c)**
> **(b c d)**
> **(c)**
> **(c d)**
> **(d)**
> **No (more) answers**
> **&.**

Listing 8.5

I included the **count-is** program to show how you can use it to limit the length of the segments.

    &which(x:x segof (a b c d e)
    land x count-is y and y LESS 4)

This will give all of the segments of **(a b c d e)** which contain fewer than four items. Or we can pursue our parsing trail and make the segments split at given elements as shown in Listing 8.6.

    &which((x|X):(x|X) segof (a b c d e)
    land (either x EQ a or x EQ c))
    (a)
    (a b)
    (a b c)
    (a b c d)
    (a b c d e)
    (c)
    (c d)
    (c d e)
    No (more) answers
    &which((x|X):(x|X) segof (the carpenter
    2walked on a mile or so) and (either x EQ a or x EQ the))
    (the)
    (the carpenter)
    (the carpenter walked)
    (the carpenter walked on)
    (the carpenter walked on a)
    (the carpenter walked on a mile)
    (the carpenter walked on a mile or)
    (the carpenter walked on a mile or so)
    (a)
    (a mile)
    (a mile or)
    (a mile or so)
    No (more) answers
    &.

Listing 8.6

EXERCISE 8.6

You will have noticed that all of the splitting-up or segmentation of lists which we have done so far has kept the elements in the order of the original list. One activity which we sometimes indulge in, either in classroom activities, or in completing football pools coupons, or working out word-search puzzles, is the permutation of lists. A permutation is a rearrangement of the elements of a list.

    Write a micro-PROLOG routine to produce all of the permutations — i.e. all of the possible arrangements — of a list. It can be done using just **append-to** and **del**. I use the **perm-of** program during the next few pages of the book, so that's where you'll find the solution. A run of my solution is:

    &which(x:x perm-of (a b c))
    (a b c)
    (a c b)

(b a c)
(b c a)
(c a b)
(c b a)
No (more) answers
&.

8.7   Links of a chain and the **forall** operator

It is sometimes useful to think of a list being divided up into a sequence of adjacent pairs of items. For example if you had a set of lists in your data-base which described the various lines of the London Underground system, and each station in a line was an item in a list, then it might be critical if you wished to plan a certain journey by Underground to know which stations were next to each other. In the same way your lists might describe paths through a maze, or through a game of dungeons and dragons, where knowledge as to whether you could pass from one situation to a neighbouring one may be critical. I think of lists in these circumstances as **chains**, and of each pair of neighbouring items as **links** in these chains.

You will readily see that the rule for **link-in** is almost identical to **item-in**, except that we are now concerned with pairs of items rather than individual ones:

 &list all
 (X Y) link-in (X Y | Z)
 (X Y) link-in (Z | x) if
   (X Y) link-in x
 &which(x y:(x y) link-in (a b c d e))
 a b
 b c
 c d
 d e
 No (more) answers
 &.

We can extend this idea by picking out links where the first of the pair is lower in value than the second:

 &which(x y:(x y) link-in (3 1 7 4 9 6) and x LESS y)
 1 7
 4 9
 No (more) answers
 &.

If, instead of the **LESS** operator, you use the **lesseq** rule which you wrote as an answer to Exercise 4.2, then you can include the possibility of neighbours having equal values, and edge towards defining an 'ordered' list:

 &list all
 (X Y) link-in (X Y | Z)
 (X Y) link-in (Z | x) if
   (X Y) link-in x
 X lesseq X
 X lesseq Y if
   X LESS Y

&which(x y:(x y) link-in (1 5 3 8 8 9 2) and x lesseq y)
1 5
3 8
8 8
8 9
No (more) answers
&.

If a whole list is ordered then all of the links must obey the **lesseq** relationship. So, we want to test whether the **lesseq** relationship holds 'for all' of the links in the chain. The micro-PROLOG operator **forall** copes with just this sort of situation, and is used in the following way:

&list ordered
X ordered if
        (forall(Y Z) link-in X then Y lesseq Z)
&is((1 3 5 7) ordered)
YES
&is((1 7 3 5 4) ordered)
NO
&is((a d e f k l) ordered)
YES
&is((a d b j e f) ordered)
NO
&.

8.8   The naive sort

We now have all of the ingredients to sort a list of items into ascending order. The **perm-of** routine shown in Listing 8.7 lets us pick out all of the arrangements of items in a list, so all we have to do is to pick out the one for which the items are ordered.

Methods of sorting lists of items into numerical or alphabetical order is a whole study in itself. The 'naive' sort which we have just looked at would certainly not be used as a practical sorting procedure. Sorting methods are quite complicated, and in part depend on the circumstances of the particular data processing task involved. To study these methods is out of place in an introductory book of this nature. But to try out some of the techniques which you have acquired in this chapter you could try the following exercise.

EXERCISE 8.7

In competitions and quizzes one engaging question comes in the form 'How many words can you make out of the word AMSTERDAM?' You have the techniques to start such an investigation, in that you can derive the various combinations of letters, and cut these up into segments to form 3-letter, 4-letter etc. combinations and so on. So, by a 'brute force and ignorance' type of approach you ought to be able to generate all possible combinations and then visually pick out those combinations which are actually words.

Try it! You will find that the amusing quiz game also becomes an absorbing programming problem. Firstly you have to write the rules, and then you will find yourself faced with what is dramatically referred to as the **combination**

```
&list all
() perm-of ()
(X|Y) perm-of Z if
      del(X Z x) and
      Y perm-of x
(() X) append-to X
((X|Y) Z) append-to (X|x) if
      (Y Z) append-to x
del(X Y Z) if
      (x (X|Y)) append-to Y and
      (x y) append-to Z
(X Y) link-in (X Y|Z)
(X Y) link-in (Z|x) if
      (X Y) link-in x
X lesseq X
X lesseq Y if
      X LESS Y
X ordered if
      (forall (Y Z) link-in X then Y lesseq Z)
&which(x:x perm-of (c b a) and x ordered)
(a b c)
No (more) answers
&which(x:x perm-of (1 3 7 4 9) and x ordered)
(1 3 4 7 9)
No (more) answers
&.
```

Listing 8.7

explosion, i.e. when micro-PROLOG tries to find solutions it keeps track of its trial solutions and by so doing the number of solution attempts soon fills even the largest micro's memory. You will find that it will pay you to tackle the problem in a series of stages, 3-letter words first, then 4-letter and 5-letter and so on, or even to store intermediate solutions as I suggest in tackling the routes problem for the London Underground in Chapter 9.

EXERCISE 8.8*

One general type of program which is frequently required in any language is to sort items into order, usually either ascending alphabetical or numerical order. There are many ways of sorting data and even more books written which devote large tracts to this problem.

You will already have glimpsed ways of sorting the items of a list into order from the work done in this chapter. One method is to find the lowest value in a list and then exchange this value with that at the first position in the list, then find the lowest value of the remaining items in the list and move it to the second position, and so on through the list. This method is called the **interchange** method. If you understand this clearly then try writing the program.

A slightly different method is known as the **bubble** sort. If you look at a list of numbers along a line of text, consider the left-hand end as the low end, and the right as high. Think of the list as a number of adjacent pairs of items as in the program we wrote for **link-in**, and for each pair find the larger of the two values and move it to be the right-hand item of the pair. The effect of this process is to move the largest value to the right-hand end of the list in the first pass through the list, the next highest to its highest position in the next pass and so on. See the effect on the following list which I have deliberately chosen as in reverse order:

(4 3 2 1) to start,
(3 2 1 4) 4 bubbles through the list on the first pass,
(2 1 3 4) 3 bubbles to its correct position on the second pass,
(1 2 3 4) 2 bubbles to its correct position on the third pass.

My version of this program is shown in the Answers. The process ends, of course, when the list is 'ordered' for which we already have a routine. A slight problem arises, however, because the program does not 'know' that there is only one ordered list, and goes off looking for others. Anyway, let me not spoil the fun for you before you have tried it for yourself.

9

A simple maze model

9.1 Introduction

My aim in this chapter is to devise one program which takes the idea of finding your way through a maze, and then use it as a general framework or model for looking at a wide range of problems, such as writing an adventure game, or looking at the schedule for a program of work, or plotting a route through the London Underground or similar system, or tracing food chains through a food web, and on to showing that the maze model can be 'opened out' to solve 'tree' type problems such as the widely quoted ancestral tree.

The programming ideas are fairly straight-forward, but a few new techniques will emerge. I will concentrate on showing how a program can be systematically built up by collecting a suitable set of your own routines, so that I can draw simple comparisons between these and the larger modules associated with micro-PROLOG, which I will describe in the last chapter of the book.

9.2 The general maze model

The maze or board shown in Fig. 9.1 has associated with it a very simple rule which is shown in the inset to the figure, namely that you can move from one square of the board, or position in the maze, to the next by moving only in an easterly (E),

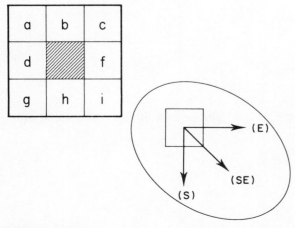

Fig. 9.1 BOARD1

southerly (S) or south-easterly (SE) direction. So the board and the rule associated with it are very simple. But as we shall see very soon, this will keep the data description of the board to manageable proportions, especially when we look at a slightly more complex board shown in Fig. 9.2, and it will not let us get into unending loops in the program, i.e. by finding a solution which just goes round and round one section of the maze indefinitely.

The basic data which describe the board and its rule could very well be expressed as a list, but I resist this temptation because it would make the initial program too complicated, and store the board simply as statements like:

    a links-to b, a links-to d, b links-to c, b links-to f

and so on for the whole of the board.

If the relationship between each cell of the board and its neighbour is thought of as a link, then why not think of routes through the board as chains. The object of the programs in this part of the book is to find all of the routes through the maze, or over the board, or in our programming terms as chains with given starting and finishing points. You will readily follow the action of the first basic program, because we broached a very similar problem in the last chapter. Listing 9.1 — **Chain1** — is followed by the BOARD1 data-base.

```
&list all
(X Y) chain1 ( ) if
      X links-to Y
(X Y) chain1 (Z|x) if
      X links-to Z and
      (Z Y) chain1 x
a links-to b
a links-to d
b links-to c
b links-to f
c links-to f
d links-to h
d links-to g
f links-to i
g links-to h
h links-to i
&.
```

Listing 9.1   chain1 and the **BOARD1** data-base

To find those routes between the first and last points in the maze we would have to ask:

```
&which(a x i:(a i) chain1 x)
a (b c f) i
a (b f) i
a (d h) i
a (d g h) i
No (more) answers
&.
```

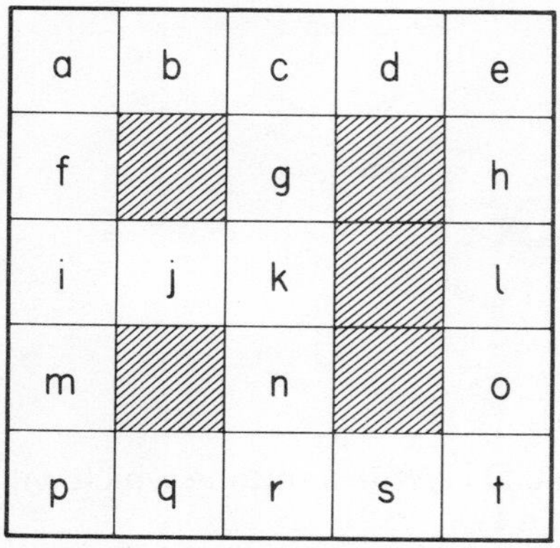

Fig. 9.2   BOARD2

The routes do not have to pass from a to i in Fig. 9.1, or a to t in Fig. 9.2, but may pass from any point upper/left to another lower/right, as shown by the following query:

&**which(a x h:(a h) chain1 x)**
a (d) h
a (d g) h
No (more) answers
&.

Or, indeed, we may wish to find out whether a route exists or not:

&**is((d i) chain1 x)**
YES
&**is((d c) chain1 x)**
NO
&.

From the above queries you can see how the rule works. The chain is seen to be the group of links between the two cells given in the query. So, the first match for the pattern **(a i) chain1 x** is:

   a   (b c f)   i
  first **chain1** last

The first sentence in the rule:

(X Y) chain1 ( ) if X links-to Y

says that if **X** and **Y** are adjacent cells, i.e. they are linked, then there is no intermediate chain, and so the chain is represented by an empty list.
   The second sentence of the rule:

(X Y) chain1 (Z|x) if X links-to Z and (Z Y) chain1 x

says that if **X links-to Z** and first **Z** and last **Y** has intermediate chain **x**, then first **X** and last **Y** has intermediate chain **(Z|x)**. I have attempted to show this in diagrammatic form in Fig. 9.3.

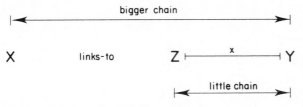

Fig. 9.3   Second sentence of the chain1 rule

EXERCISE 9.1

The **chain1** rule has left the chain in the form **a (b c f) i**. Write a routine which will gather these elements into a single list — e.g. **(a b c f i)**.

You will find the solution to this exercise wrapped up in the next program, but before we move on to that let's look at some simple guidelines for building up programs.

Listing 9.1 has two parts: the first the chain rule; and the next the board data-base which gives all of the links between cells on the board. Having entered this program and checked that it worked, I then saved it to make sure that I did not lose my work so far. So that I could use the two parts separately I first killed the chain rule and saved the board data-base with the file name BOARD1. Then I killed that remainder of the program, and reloaded the whole program again, killed the board data-base this time, and then saved the remainder under the name CHAIN1. I then had the BOARD1 and CHAIN1 programs in separate files on disk.

It is good practice when programming in micro-PROLOG to have the various parts of a program arranged in the order in which they will be called into service when the program is working. The problem with just adding rules to an existing program, is that you end up with rules in the 'wrong' order, and this can cause problems when the program runs, especially if there are several recursive loops within it. For example, had I not saved BOARD1 and CHAIN1 separately, and just carried on entering the **chain2** and **ask-for** routines which you will see below, then these would have occurred at the end of the program, after the BOARD1 data-base. To have the parts of the program in the wrong order also makes checking it much more difficult, if it does not work quite as well as you expected the first time it ran.

To add the first and last points into the list we need the ubiquitous **append-to** routine. Also to make the program a little more interactive, I will include an **ask-for** routine which just asks the user to input which starting and finishing points he/she is interested in. So, start off with **kill all** to ensure that the work-space is completely clear, and then enter the two segments of program listed below:

```
&list all
chain2 X if
        Y ask-for Z and
        (Y Z) chain1 x and
        ((Y) x) append-to y and
        (y (Z)) append-to X
X ask-for Y if
        P (Enter starting point :) and
        X R and
        P (Enter finishing point :) and
        Y R
```

The first and last points in the chain are added into a list representing the whole chain by the three lines:

(Y Z) chain1 x

which names the three parts of the chain,

((Y) x) append-to y

which turns the first point **Y** into a list **(Y)** and appends it to the chain **x**, and names it **y**, and

(y (Z)) append-to X

which appends the last point to the list **y** which we have just made.

You have always to keep clearly in your mind that **append-to** appends two lists, so we had to turn the starting and finishing points into lists each containing only one item, before joining them with **append-to**.

You are now at the point where you have the rules **chain2** and **ask-for** in your work-space. To make the program work you now have to load in the file you saved called CHAIN1, and your version of **append-to**, followed by BOARD1. These files will just be added on to the end of your work-space each time you load, so they will now be joined on to the end of **chain2** and **ask-for** in the order in which they are called when the program runs. The complete program (Listing 9.2) is shown below because it is essential to the discussions in the next few pages, except that I have not included the **links-to** data-base which was saved in BOARD1, just to save space in the text.

```
&list all
chain2 X if
        Y ask-for Z and
        (Y Z) chain1 x and
        ((Y) x) append-to y and
        (y (Z)) append-to X
X ask-for Y if
        P (Enter starting point :) and
        X R and
        P (Enter finishing point :) and
        Y R
(X Y) chain1 ( ) if
        X links-to Y
(X Y) chain1 (Z|x) if
        X links-to Z and
        (Z Y) chain1 x
(( ) X) append-to X
((X|Y) Z) append-to (X|x) if
        (Y Z) append-to x

... BOARD1 data-base ...
```

Listing 9.2   chain2, ask-for, chain1 and **append-to** followed by the BOARD1 data-base

You can see the effect of this program by entering the following query.

&which(x:chain2 x)
Enter starting point :a
Enter finishing point :i
(a b c f i)
(a b f i)
(a d h i)
(a d g h i)
No (more) answers
&.

Listing 9.2 without the BOARD1 data-base will form the core of future programs which we will write, so delete the data-base from it by saying **kill links-to**. If you now save what is left, then you will have saved as PROGRAM2 (say) the program shown above without the data-base.

You will have realised by now that the board stored as BOARD1 was only to be used to test the programs we have written, but is not very interesting in its own right. So, clear your work-space by saying **kill all**, and enter the data-base for BOARD2 shown in Fig. 9.2. When you see the listing of BOARD2 it looks a bit of a marathon, but it does not take long to enter using the **accept** command, when you only have to enter the two letters of the adjacent cells in brackets.

The data-base BOARD2 is shown below, but to save space in the text I have shown four data sentences per line.

a links-to b	**a links-to f**	**b links-to c**	**b links-to g**
c links-to d	**c links-to g**	**d links-to e**	**d links-to h**
f links-to i	**f links-to j**	**g links-to k**	**h links-to l**
i links-to j	**i links-to m**	**j links-to k**	**j links-to n**
k links-to n	**l links-to o**	**m links-to p**	**m links-to q**
n links-to r	**n links-to s**	**o links-to t**	**p links-to q**
q links-to r	**r links-to s**	**s links-to t**	

The BOARD2 data-base

If you now save this data-base as BOARD2 and then clear the work-space with **kill all**, and then re-load PROGRAM2 followed by BOARD2, you can use PROGRAM2 to find ways through the new board or maze.

The following query gives all of the alternative paths through a section of this new maze:

&which(x:chain2 x)
Enter starting point :i
Enter finishing point :s
(i j k n s)
(i j k n r s)
(i j n s)
(i j n r s)
(i m p q r s)
(i m q r s)
No (more) answers
&.

Whereas the following query finds all of the possible paths through the maze:

&which(x:chain2 x)
Enter starting point :a
Enter finishing point :t
(a b c d h l o t)
(a b c g k n r s t)
(a b c g k n s t)
(a b g k n r s t)
(a b g k n s t)
(a f i j k n r s t)
(a f i j k n s t)
(a f i j n r s t)
(a f i j n s t)
(a f i m p q r s t)
(a f i m q r s t)
(a f j k n r s t)
(a f j k n s t)
(a f j n r s t)
(a f j n s t)
No (more) answers
&.

9.3 Ancestral tree

So PROGRAM2 which consists of the collection of routines:

chain2
ask-for
chain1
append-to

finds the various paths through a maze, and presents them in the form of a list. You will have realised by now that the BOARD data-bases which describe the structure of the mazes may be changed to suit a particular application, and that the maze is only one particular type of linked structure for which the program has a use.

The problem of tracing a chain of ancestors through an ancestral tree is one application which is often found in texts on micro-PROLOG. Here the maze becomes a tree. The Royal ancestral tree from Queen Victoria to the present day is shown in Fig. 9.4, with the letters (a) (b) (c) . . . (q) showing the **nodes** in the tree structure which are analogous to the cells in the mazes which we have used before. Fig. 9.5 picks out this tree skeleton more clearly, and this 'BOARD' is described in the data-base shown in BOARD3.

So, if you load PROGRAM2 into a cleared memory, followed by the BOARD3 data-base as shown in Listing 9.3, you could carry on and interrogate it as shown.

PROGRAM2

links-to (a b) links-to (a c) links-to (c d)
links-to (d e) links-to (d f) links-to (d g)
links-to (d h) links-to (d i) links-to (f j)   The BOARD3 data-base
links-to (f k) links-to (j l) links-to (j m)
links-to (j n) links-to (j o) links-to (l p)
links-to (l q)

```
&which(x:chain2 x)
Enter starting point :a
Enter finishing point :i
(a c d i)
No (more) answers
&which(x:chain2 x)
Enter starting point :d
Enter finishing point :q
(d f j l q)
No (more) answers
&.
```

Listing 9.3

The sentences in BOARD3 have been condensed, three sentences per line, to save a little space.

We will only have the skeleton of a solution, but we can add flesh to it by adding a further data-base consisting of the details shown in Fig. 9.4 as shown below in DETAILS1.

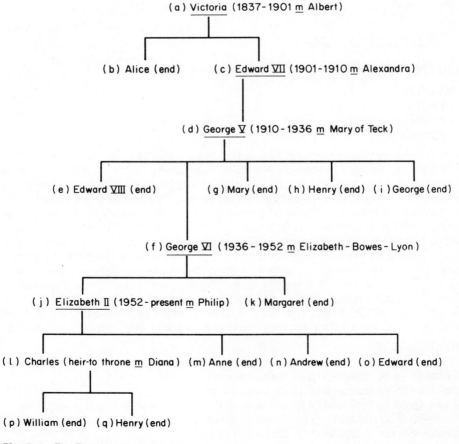

Fig. 9.4   The Royal ancestral tree

details (a (VICTORIA Q1837-1901 ALBERT))
details (b (ALICE NFD EOR))
details (c (EDWARDVII K1901-1910 ALEXANDRA))
details (d (GEORGEV K1910-1936 MARY-OF-TECK))
details (e (EDWARDVIII NFD EOR))
details (f (GEORGEVI K1936-1952 ELIZABETH-BOWES-LYON))
details (g (MARY NFD EOR))
details (h (HENRY NFD EOR))
details (i (GEORGE NFD EOR))
details (j (ELIZABETHII Q1952-PRESENT PHILIP))
details (k (MARGARET NFD EOR))
details (l (CHARLES HEIR-TO-THRONE DIANA))
details (m (ANNE NFD EOR))
details (n (ANDREW NFD EOR))
details (o (EDWARD NFD EOR))
details (p (WILLIAM NFD EOR))
details (q (HENRY NFD EOR))

The DETAILS1 data-base

As you can see I have added the details to the nodes (a b c d . . . etc. . . .) of the tree
in the form of a list of three items. In the cases where I considered that further data
is not significant I have completed the list with **NFD** and **EOR**, 'no further data' and
'end of record' respectively.

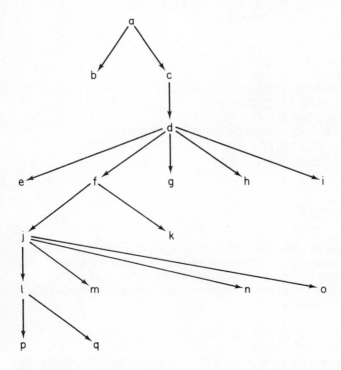

Fig. 9.5 Diagram for BOARD3

It is obvious that the items in the list of nodes for the route through the tree which is found by PROGRAM2 with BOARD3 as shown above, can be made to show the details of the royal personage at that point by calling for details from DETAILS1. So, all we need now is a routine which looks at each item in that list and goes to the **details** relation to find the appropriate list of details. I have called the routine **chain ancestors**, and the whole program will have the following form:

```
chain ancestors if
       chain2 x and
       (forall y item-in x          1a
       then y details z and         1b
            PP (z))                  1c
```

followed by

```
PROGRAM2
item-in
BOARD3
DETAILS1
```

Line 1a looks at each item in the **chain2** list, then 1b finds the details related to each item, and 1c prints out each detail list.

A run of the program would look like Listing 9.4.

```
&ancestors chain
Enter starting point :d
Enter finishing point :o
(GEORGEV K1910-1936 MARY-OF-TECK)
(GEORGEVI K1936-1952 ELIZABETH-BOWES-LYON)
(ELIZABETHII Q1952-PRESENT PHILIP)
(EDWARD NFD EOR)
&ancestors chain
Enter starting point :a
Enter finishing point :q
(VICTORIA Q1837-1901 ALBERT)
(EDWARDVII K1901-1910 ALEXANDRA)
(GEORGEV K1910-1936 MARY-OF-TECK)
(GEORGEVI K1936-1952 ELIZABETH-BOWES-LYON)
(ELIZABETHII Q1952-PRESENT PHILIP)
(CHARLES HEIR-TO-THRONE DIANA)
(HENRY NFD EOR)
&.
```

Listing 9.4

There are some further modifications which you would wish to make if you were to use the program regularly, apart from extending the detail of the data itself. You would probably wish to cut out entering the starting and finishing nodes by their board name letters (a and q in the second run above), and allow the user to enter the names of the personages involved.

EXERCISE 9.2

You could re-write this ancestral tree program replacing **links-to** with **parent-of**, and extend the data-base adding in details of your choice, such as the rare blood

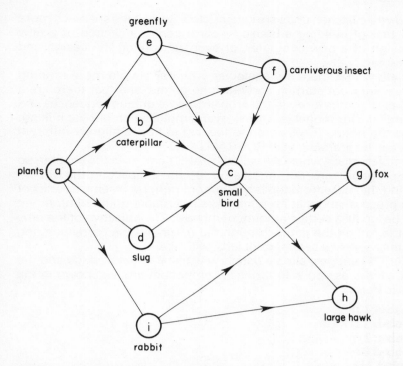

greenfly

carniverous insect

caterpillar

plants

small
bird

fox

slug

large hawk

rabbit

Fig. 9.6 Food Web. (Reproduced from *Biology by Enquiry*, Clarke, Booth et al, by kind permission of Heinemann Educational Books)

disease which was found in the male descendant line from Victoria. You might be totally dissatisfied with the whole program and wish to write one for yourself which traces an ancestral chain back from a given point, to answer a question of the form 'Who are the ancestors of Henry?', with all of the problems which attend a question which you will recognise now as being unsatisfactorily vague.

EXERCISE 9.3

Write BOARD and DETAILS data-bases for the food web diagram in Fig. 9.6, and trace the various food chains found in the web. The arrows in Fig. 9.6 have a direct functional meaning if you think of the sense of the arrows as 'provider → predator'. The output should give statements like 'plants feed caterpillars', 'greenfly feed small-birds' etc., and the DETAILS file could contain details of the relative sizes of the animals, their relative numbers, and so on. Once again you may have to re-write some of the rules to suit the way you choose to store the data.

9.4   Job scheduling

When a house is built the various phases of the building program have to be scheduled very carefully. Some parts of the construction have to be done in strict sequence, walls put up before major carpentry can be done, electrical wiring before plastering and so on. Other jobs may be done in parallel — e.g. electrical fittings made good while kitchen units are constructed. Some jobs are much more complicated than that of building a house — constructing a section of a new motorway, the design of a new computer, or even scheduling the design and production of a new car.

I hope you will allow that there are analogies with our simple maze running model, in that there are clear starting and finishing points, and that there are a multifarious number of routes through the problem, some unique sequences and other routes in parallel. Our model is a gross over-simplification but yet it is not totally unreal, and the notion leads us on to looking at how a slightly different program segment can be grafted on to PROGRAM2.

I will take the simplest maze which we called BOARD1 earlier in the chapter, so that the eventual program runs do not take up too much space in the book. I assume that running the maze from top left to bottom right represents a series of jobs in a building process, and that each job takes a certain amount of time — it could just as well be 'costs a certain amount of money'. The objective of the new program segment is to find the paths through the maze and the corresponding total times which the routes, or sequence of jobs, will take.

Linked with BOARD1 I suggest simple details which state the job stage and the time (hours, days, weeks as you will) for each component job, as shown in the DETAILS2 data-base below.

> **a details (job-a 10)**
> **b details (job-b 12)**
> **c details (job-c 7)**
> **d details (job-d 8)**
> **f details (job-f 15)**
> **g details (job-g 15)**
> **h details (job-h 6)**
> **i details (job-i 14)**

DETAILS2 data-base

EXERCISE 9.4

The problem is very similar to the previous routine which we wrote, which, as I have said, is part of the message. You have to look at each item in the list of cells, or jobs in this case, which is represented by **chain2 x**, find the details list for that cell and pick out the number which represents the time for the job, make a list of the times for each path or sequence of jobs, and then, when the list is complete, output the total of the list. It is not as complicated as it sounds when expressed in words and I suggest that you tackle it as an exercise before you carry on to my solution.

My routine has the following form:

> **schedule jobs X if**
> **chain2 Y and**
> **(forall Z item-in Y**   1a
> **then Z details x and**   1b
> **PP(x)) and**   1c
> **y isall (z:**   2a
> **x1 item-in Y and**   2b
> **x1 details (y1 z)) and**   2c
> **PP(y) and**   3a
> **PP(The total is) and**   3b
> **y total-is X**   4a

After **chain2 Y** gets the path **Y** in the form of a list, then the next sentence of the rule marked 1a 1b 1c finds the details for each item in the path and prints them out at 1c. Sentence 2 makes a list of all of the second items in the details list — note **isall (z: . . . details (y1 z))** picks out the second item **z**. Line 3a prints out this list followed by the message **The total is** at line 3b. In the run which follows the actual value is printed out as a response to the **which** query.

Before we look at a run let's make sure of the composition of the complete program. It will have the following segments:

> **schedule jobs X (as given above)**
> **PROGRAM2**
> **item-in**
> **total-is**   (exactly as in earlier chapters)
> **BOARD1**
> **DETAILS2**

A run of the program went as shown in Listing 9.5.

> **&which(x:schedule jobs x)**
> **Enter starting point :a**
> **Enter finishing point :i**
> **(job-a 10)**
> **(job-b 12)**
> **(job-c 7)**
> **(job-f 15)**
> **(job-i 14)**
> **(10 12 7 15 14)**
> **The total is**
> **58**
> **(job-a 10)**
> **(job-b 12)**
> **(job-f 15)**
> **(job-i 14)**
> **(10 12 15 14)**
> **The total is**
> **51**
> **(job-a 10)**
> **(job-d 8)**
> **(job-h 6)**
> **(job-i 14)**
> **(10 8 6 14)**
> **The total is**
> **38**
> **(job-a 10)**
> **(job-d 8)**
> **(job-g 15)**
> **(job-h 6)**
> **(job-i 14)**
> **(10 8 15 6 14)**
> **The total is**
> **53**
> **No (more) answers**
> **&.**

Listing 9.5

Yes, the program is still in a very rudimentary state because you have to scan the totals to find the minimum value of 38 in this case. If you want a challenge you could write this refinement, you will have to put the totals into a list and then use the **minimum** routines which we developed in Chapter 8. You would also have to store the details of the paths through the maze so that when you have found the minimum valued path, then you can print it out.

9.5   London Underground routes

In Fig. 9.6 I have shown a small central section of the London Underground Railway network. It will be apparent to you just how to set about entering this map as a maze-type data-base. From our experience with earlier problems of this type you will realise how many possible routes we will be able to find between different points on this map. We could enter data with a **details** relationship as above to include details of price or time taken between stops along the various routes, and continue to find the total times or prices involved in these possible journeys.

The problem I am going to solve is to find routes which involve travelling only on one of the several lines which are available and are often very confusing to the traveller. In other words to find a direct or 'no change' route. So not only do we need the map shown, but also a way of storing the information about the different lines which are shown in different colours on the published Underground maps, and this I do later in LINE1 data-base.

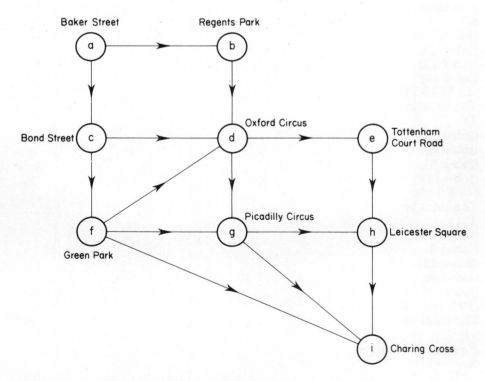

Fig. 9.7   A section of the London Underground

I am also concerned that the programs at this stage of the book tend to get quite long and so more and more difficult to follow, so I am going to show how you can write your first attempt at solving a problem in two separate programs. We need a way of saving the results of one program run so that we can use them with another program. To be specific I am going to find all of the routes between two stations — Bond Street and Charing Cross in this case — and then add them to the data-base and then save them for future use.

First load in PROGRAM2 to an empty work-space followed by BOARD4 which is the map of the Underground in our **links-to** form.

PROGRAM2

links-to (a b)	**links-to (a c)**	**links-to (b d)**
links-to (c d)	**links-to (c f)**	**links-to (d e)**
links-to (d g)	**links-to (e h)**	**links-to (f d)**
links-to (f g)	**links-to (f i)**	**links-to (g h)**
links-to (g i)	**links-to (h i)**	

The BOARD4 data-base

Once again I have shown three sentences to a line to save some space. Now continue:

```
&all((route x):chain2 x and (route x) add)
Enter starting point :c
Enter finishing point :i
(route (c d e h i))
(route (c d g i))
(route (c d g h i))
(route (c f i))
(route (c f d e h i))
(route (c f d g i))
(route (c f d g h i))
(route (c f g h i))
(route (c f g h i))
No (more) answers
&.
```

If you now list **route** you will find that the **route** data-base has been added on to the end of the program in your work-space, in the form:

```
&list route
route (c d e h i)
route (c d g i)
```

and so on.

I then cleared the other relationships out of the work-space, with: **kill chain2, kill chain1, kill ask-for, kill append-to, kill links-to** leaving just the **route** data-base in the machine's memory, and then I saved it as ROUTE1.

You will have realised how powerful this last technique is. The statement:

&all((route x):chain2 x and (route x) add)

defines a new relationship **route** and **(route x) add** adds the values found for this relationship to the data-base. This means that you now have a way of storing the results which your programs produce permanently in your program. In a very crude way you can think of the program as learning (retaining) the results of its own processing. Anyway, we now have stored the results of a query on the program which comprises PROGRAM2 and the Underground data-base BOARD4.

The next stage in solving the problem of choosing those routes which are direct or no-change journeys, is to write relationships which define the various lines of the Underground system. The following LINE1 data-base will do:

> **&list line**
> **line (B (Bakerloo (a b d g i)))**
> **line (C (Central (c d e)))**
> **line (J (Jubilee (a c f i)))**
> **line (N (Northern (e h i)))**
> **line (P (Piccadilly (f g h)))**
> **line (V (Victoria (f d)))**
> **&.**

The LINE1 data-base

Now if these are the direct routes provided by the various lines then all we have to do is to find whether a route which occurs in the ROUTE1 data-base is a segment of the list for one of the lines given above.

You will recall that we wrote a program to find the segment of a list of characters in Chapter 8. So, we can lift the relationship **segof** straight out of that chapter, and build up a program from sentences of:

> **segof**
> **ROUTE1**
> **LINE1**

which when interrogated will give the following response:

> **&which(x z line:route x and line (y (z X)) and x segof X)**
> **(c f i) Jubilee line**
> **No (more) answers**
> **&.**

This does seem rather a stark response after all that hard work, and you can give a little more flesh to the bones by adding a **details** data-base — DETAILS3.

> **&list details**
> **a details Baker-St**
> **b details Regents-Pk**
> **c details Bond-St**
> **d details Oxford-Cir**
> **e details Tottenham-Ct-Rd**
> **f details Green-Pk**
> **g details Piccadilly-Cir**
> **h details Leicester-Sq**
> **i details Charing-Cr**
> **&.**

The DETAILS3 data-base

The following program and query will elicit a more realistic result:

> **segof**
> **item-in**
> **ROUTE1**
> **LINE1**
> **DETAILS3**

&which(Y on the z line:route x and
lline(y (z X)) and x segof X and
1Y is all(Z:x1 item-in x and x1 details Z))
(Bond-St Green-Pk Charing-Cr) on the Jubilee line
No (more) answers
&.

EXERCISE 9.5

This is really just a series of suggestions to polish up and make more realistic the above program. Yes, I could have written the two routines together all in one long program — so you could try that if you wish. Further you could write the above **which** query as rules at the top of this large program in the form of **forall** loops. In its present form if a route is chosen which has no direct or straight through journey then all the above query would do is reply with the maddening **No (more) answers**. So there is room for you to improve on this very rudimentary first attempt, with a rule which either finds the direct journeys or responds with 'There is no straight through journey possible.'

10
Perspectives

10.1 Introduction

It is tempting in a book like this just to continue with more and more complicated programming, to develop in detail a games, business or educational program. It has been my experience that readers often use a book to reach a certain point of competence in a language, and then after that point they wish to develop programs which are of interest to them, not those which have been chosen by the author of a book. Further, if you chose to describe programs which use the file-handling or graphics facilities of a particular system for example, it is these very features which have changed before the book is published, or about which it is very difficult to generalise to make the text meaningful for readers of different systems.

I have chosen to lean back and try to take an overview of the language as a whole, to show that micro-PROLOG provides a whole working environment for the user. I take a brief, but I hope meaningful, look at the Standard Syntax of the language, which is about the lowest level at which you can use it. By 'lowest' I mean 'least sophisticated'. You have had nine chapters of the next level up, namely the SIMPLE form of micro-PROLOG. The next part of the chapter looks in detail at the modules which are provided with the system, usually on disk; these are programs which are prepared to help the user in using the language to the full, and in his/her own program development. Finally, I take a very brief look at how you may continue your micro-PROLOG activities.

The fact that micro-PROLOG offers you these different working levels is one of the reasons why you should feel that you are operating in a whole working environment, rather than just using a particular programming language. The purpose of the programmer should be to raise the level of this environment, to serve as fully as possible a particular application.

10.2 Standard syntax

The Standard Syntax of micro-PROLOG gives us a more primitive version of the language, which is on the one hand more restrictive in that it has a much narrower range of commands and operators, but on the other has a simplicity which may very well appeal to you. Without SIMPLE in the work-space there is more room for larger programs written in Standard Syntax, and more room to load in and run the standard modules, such as a TRACE module which we found to be too big to be effective in the 48k RAM of the BBC Model B micro. Standard Syntax programs should run more quickly than those written in SIMPLE.

When you have entered micro-PROLOG with the appropriate command — e.g. ***PROLOG** on the BBC system — you find yourself at the **&.** prompt, and can start to enter data immediately:

&((EEC BELGIUM 9.9 11.8))
&.

The **&.** means that the system has accepted the data in the form given, which you will recognise as a list. **&(. . .)** is the way you enter data, acting like **add** in the SIMPLE dialect, and **(** data list **)** is the list of data which has been entered, so the complete form is **&((** data list **))**. Let's add one more data list:

&((EEC FRANCE 54 213))
&.

The data, by the way, says that Belgium and France are EEC countries, with populations 9.9 and 54 millions respectively, and areas 11.8 and 213 thousand square miles. There is no **is** nor **which** operator in Standard Syntax; the standard way that you ask questions is by using the **?** operator at the **&.** prompt:

&?((EEC FRANCE X Y))
&.

The query asks 'is there a record with the form **EEC FRANCE** followed by two other values?'. The receipt of the **&.** prompt after the query signals that the query was successful. On the other hand:

&?((EEC UK X Y))
?
&.

asks about a data list which is not in the data-base and receives the response **?** followed by **&.** which means that the system cannot find such a data list. So the form of the query is **&?(. . .)**, where the inner data list may contain some variables, and the responses are two-fold: **&.** for 'success' of the query, and **?** followed by **&.** which denotes the 'failure' of the query. Variables are used in the same way in Standard Syntax as they are in SIMPLE.

I will carry on now and enter four more records for this data-base, so that when listed it looks like:

&LIST ALL
((EEC BELGIUM 9.9 11.8))
((EEC FRANCE 54 213))
((EEC ITALY 56.5 131))
((EEC NETHERLANDS 14.2 13.5))
((EEC UK 55.9 93))
((EEC W-GERMANY 61.7 96))
&.

As we saw with SIMPLE **is** queries, it is all very well knowing that a question has met with success or failure, but usually you wish to locate and display items of data. In Standard Syntax you have to make up your displays, or print-outs using the ubiquitous **PP** operator. Yes, you will have begun to realise that the operators which we used with capital letters in SIMPLE, are directly transferrable to Standard Syntax, and you will now appreciate why I made so much use of this particular operator earlier in the book.

Remember that the most important feature of micro-PROLOG is its forward searching and backtracking mode of execution. Look at the following query with its 'pretty-print' output, and try and convince yourself that you understand how it does what it does, before you read my explanation:

```
&?((EEC X Y Z)(PP X)(EEC A B C))
BELGIUM
FRANCE
ITALY
NETHERLANDS
UK
W-GERMANY
?
&.
```

You will remember that we said earlier that **PP** is a command which is always true. Now, I add the restriction that it is a **single match** command, so that in any single pass through a query it can receive and print out a value once only.

Firstly the system tries to match **(EEC X Y Z)** against the data base and succeeds; X=BELGIUM in this first match and this value is passed on to **(PP X)** and is printed out. Then the system meets **(EEC A B C)** and tries to match that against a record in its memory and cannot, so the match fails and backtracking occurs back to **(PP X)** which has made the one discharge which it is allowed, and so it fails too. So, backtracking occurs again and **(EEC X Y Z)** is tried for the second time. This attempt is successful with X=FRANCE, which is passed on to **(PP X)** which discharges this value, and on to **(EEC A B C)** which fails and results in more backtracking through the rest of the data-base.

You have to realise that **(EEC A B C)** is a **dummy** data record. **A**, **B** and **C** are not variables but 'possible' data values, whose values we know will not actually be in the data-base. The presence of this dummy list in the query is solely to force the backtracking process. The two following queries should add to the illustration.

```
&?((EEC X Y Z)(PP X)(EQ X ITALY))
BELGIUM
FRANCE
ITALY
&?((EEC X Y Z)(PP X)(EQ X ZZZZ))
BELGIUM
FRANCE
ITALY
NETHERLANDS
UK
W-GERMANY
?
&.
```

In the first query **(EQ X ITALY)** still forces the backtracking process, but only until the record is found in which X=ITALY. The outcome is a success and so no **?** appears after the print-out of **ITALY**. In the second query there is no record where X=ZZZZ, so **(EQ X ZZZZ)** forces the backtracking, and the search ends in failure, shown by the **?** after **W-GERMANY**, but in the process has caused all of the countries' names to be displayed. Refer to the trace of this program in Listing 10.1.

I used the operator **EQ** in this last example, and you will not be surprised to learn that **SUM**, **TIMES** and **LESS** can also be used in a similar way to how we used them in SIMPLE. You will see some of these in use in the following rules.

You can enter rules into the system in a similar way to entering data, with one or

```
&LOAD"TRACE"
&??((EEC X Y Z)(PP X)(EQ X ZZZZ))
(1) (EEC X Y Z) trace?Y
(1) matches clause 1
(1) solved (EEC BELGIUM 9.9 11.8)
(2) (PP BELGIUM)
BELGIUM
(2) solved (PP BELGIUM)
(3) (EQ BELGIUM ZZZZ)
(3) failing (EQ BELGIUM ZZZZ)
(2) failing (PP BELGIUM)
(1) matches clause 2
(1) solved (EEC FRANCE 54 213)
(2) (PP FRANCE)
FRANCE
(2) solved (PP FRANCE)
(3) (EQ FRANCE ZZZZ)
(3) failing (EQ FRANCE ZZZZ)
(2) failing (PP FRANCE)
(1) matches clause 3
(1) solved (EEC ITALY 56.5 131)
(2) (PP ITALY)
ITALY
(2) solved (PP ITALY)
(3) (EQ ITALY ZZZZ)
(3) failing (EQ ITALY ZZZZ)
(2) failing (PP ITALY)
(1) matches clause 4
(1) solved (EEC NETHERLANDS 14.2 13.5)
(2) (PP NETHERLANDS)
NETHERLANDS
(2) solved (PP NETHERLANDS)
(3) (EQ NETHERLANDS ZZZZ)
(3) failing (EQ NETHERLANDS ZZZZ)
(2) failing (PP NETHERLANDS)
(1) matches clause 5
(1) solved (EEC UK 55.9 93)
(2) (PP UK)
UK
(2) solved (PP UK)
(3) (EQ UK ZZZZ)
(3) failing (EQ UK ZZZZ)
(2) failing (PP UK)
(1) matches clause 6
(1) solved (EEC W-GERMANY 61.7 96)
(2) (PP W-GERMANY)
W-GERMANY
(2) solved (PP W-GERMANY)
(3) (EQ W-GERMANY ZZZZ)
(3) failing (EQ W-GERMANY ZZZZ)
(2) failing (PP W-GERMANY)
(1) failing (EEC X Y Z)
?
&.
```

Trace Listing 10.1

more lists inside the enter brackets **&(. . .)**, except that now the lists will contain variables. In the first rule below I wish to define a 'high-population' as one of the EEC countries which has a population greater than 20 million. The rule which would be added to the above data-base would look like:

&((HIGH-POP X)(EEC X Y Z)(LESS 20 Y))
&.

You have to understand that the rule has the implied structure:

(HIGH-POP X) 'if' **(EEC X Y Z)** 'and' **(LESS 20 Y)**

Between the first and second bracketed terms you imagine there to be an 'if' as in SIMPLE, and between the rest of the bracketed terms you imagine an 'and'. Now you can use the dummy variables approach with this rule to get the desired search through the whole file:

&?((HIGH-POP X)(PP X)(HIGH-POP A))
FRANCE
ITALY
UK
W-GERMANY
?
&.

The following rule picks out those countries whose populaton is less than 20 millions:

&((LOW-POP X)(EEC X Y Z)(LESS Y 20))
&?((LOW-POP X)(PP X)(LOW-POP A))
BELGIUM
NETHERLANDS
?
&.

To show that it is possible to write an interesting program fairly quickly in Standard Syntax, I will enter a rule to find the population densities in units of millions of people per thousand square miles:

&((POP-DENS (X x))(EEC X Y Z)(TIMES x Z Y))
&?((POP-DENS (X x))(PP (X x))(POP-DENS A 1)))
(BELGIUM 0.838983051)
(FRANCE 0.253521127)
(ITALY 0.43129771)
(NETHERLANDS 1.05185185)
(UK 0.601075269)
(W-GERMANY 0.642708333)
?
&.

The rules have gone into the data-base in the opposite order to our earlier experiences with SIMPLE, so that the last rule entered is now at the top of the file:

&LIST ALL
((POP-DENS (X Y))
      (EEC X Z x)
      (TIMES Y x Z))

```
((LOW-POP X)
      (EEC X Y Z)
      (LESS Y 20))
((HIGH-POP X)
      (EEC X Y Z)
      (LESS 20 Y))
((EEC BELGIUM 9.9 11.8))
```
. . . and so on through the rest of the data

The dummy data record approach to searching through a data-base may have simplicity to recommend it, but it is rather primitive for a high-level language. Is there not a **forall** type operator as there is in SIMPLE? Would the dummy data approach let you handle recursive rules? The answer to the first question is 'Yes', and to the second is 'No' not in general terms. There is a **FORALL** operator in Standard Syntax but not in the ROM based program; it has to be loaded in from the **logic module** in a file called LOGIC. This module also contains routines for **NOT**, **IF** and **ISALL**. So, with the above data-base still in the machine you can proceed:

```
&LOAD"LOGIC"
&?((FORALL((HIGH-POP X))((PP X))))
FRANCE
ITALY
UK
W-GERMANY
&.
```

Notice that the evaluation now does not end with the **?** **&.** sequence, for the search through the data has not ended in failure. Note also the use of the double brackets in the query.

Let's clear the data-base which we have been using out of the work-space with **KILL ALL**, and briefly look at some familiar recursive rules in Standard Syntax. If you had entered our old favourite **item-in** a listing would look like:

```
&LIST ALL
((ITEM-IN X (X|Y)))
((ITEM-IN X (Y|Z))
      (ITEM-IN X Z))
&?((ITEM-IN X (A B C))
A
&LOAD"LOGIC"
&?((FORALL((ITEM-IN X (A B C)))((PP X))))
A
B
C
&.
```

I said earlier that without SIMPLE in the work-space you have more room for your programs. You will remember that I said that when you use Simtrac to trace the operation of a program in the BBC Model B, you soon run out of memory. The Standard Syntax equivalent of Simtrac is the TRACE module, which is stored in a file of that name. This gives a slightly simpler trace of a program, and of course can trace longer program runs because of the greater RAM space that it has available.

Clear the work-space and enter a Standard Syntax version of **appends-to**, and then list and run:

```
&LIST ALL
((APPEND ( ) X X))
((APPEND (X|Y) Z (X|x))
      (APPEND Y Z x))
&?((APPEND (A B C) (D E) X)(PP X))
(A B C D E)
&.
```

To see what happens in the evaluation of this rule:

```
&LOAD"TRACE"
&??((APPEND (A B C) (D E) X)(PP X))
```

The trace is shown in Trace Listing 10.2 and I hope you will agree that it does show what is happening very clearly — much more clearly than in the trace of **append-to** in Listing 6.7. Yes, you do have to enter **??**; one to start the query and the other to start the trace, is one way of thinking of it.

```
&??((APPEND (A B C) (D E) X) (PP X))
(1) (APPEND (A B C) (D E) X) trace?Y
(1) matches clause 2
(1 1) (APPEND (B C) (D E) X) trace?Y
(1 1) matches clause 2
(1 1 1) (APPEND (C) (D E) X) trace?Y
(1 1 1) matches clause 2
(1 1 1 1) (APPEND ( ) (D E) X) trace?Y
(1 1 1 1) matches clause 1
(1 1 1 1) solved (APPEND ( ) (D E) (D E))
(1 1 1) solved (APPEND (C) (D E) (C D E))
(1 1) solved (APPEND (B C) (D E) (B C D E))
(1) solved (APPEND (A B C) (D E) (A B C D E))
(2) (PP (A B C D E))
(A B C D E)
(2) solved (PP (A B C D E))
&.
```

Listing 10.2

I have included in Trace Listing 10.1 a trace of the:

((EEC X Y Z)(PP X)(EQ X ZZZZ))

query, because it does show the backtracking, and the function of the dummy **(EQ X ZZZZ)** and single evaluation of **(PP X)**, so very clearly.

EXERCISE 10.1

If you have taken a liking to the Standard Syntax, then I do not need to say that a very instructive activity now would be to go back to the exercises and examples in the earlier part of the book, and re-write them in Standard Syntax using the tracing facility as widely as is needed to clarify any worries you may have about how the language works.

10.3   The language and its modules

In the earlier part of the book I deliberately avoided some of the more pedantic ways of describing the structure of micro-PROLOG itself, because I feel that worrying about the finer points of the language at an early stage can detract from its essential simplicity. Now we have looked at the Standard Syntax version of the language, we are in a better position to look at the finer details on the one hand, and on the other we should be better able to appreciate the role played in the language by its **modules**. One of the major strengths of micro-PROLOG is its extensibility and it is mainly through its modules that it is extensible.

The rest of the chapter is concerned with taking a bird's-eye view of the language, from its inner structure out through its modules so to speak, to form a succinct survey and base from which, hopefully, you will choose to extend your use of the language. If nothing else it should allow you to find your way a little more easily through the manuals which accompany the software, which are often rather daunting because of the level of detail contained in them. I apologise in advance to the academics for taking a little poetic licence with some of the ideas, for the sake of general simplicity.

10.3.1   TOKENS AND TERMS

The first two terms which you encounter are **tokens** and **terms**. Broadly speaking tokens are those characters which appear on the keyboard of the computer for which the software has been provided — not just the letters and digits, but also the special characters |, *, /, % and so on. The special characters have not been used much in this book, but have greater significance when you are concerned with file-handling and screen graphics on a particular system.

These tokens may be grouped together to make terms which have some significance for the language. Terms are referred to rather grandly (or obscurely) as **syntactic objects**. I called them words earlier in the book and they come in four main types: numbers, constants, variables and lists. I have discussed these in earlier chapters: numbers being numeric terms which are used for calculations; constants can be either terms which are items of data or the relationship words themselves; variables are represented by terms formed by starting with one of the tokens x, y, z, X, Y or Z, or one of those six characters followed immediately with a positive integer.

The list is a very important type of term, for it may itself be a collection of terms enclosed between the tokens (and), with the enclosed terms separated by spaces and the special symbol |. The | is the only data constructor in micro-PROLOG and divides the list into a **head** which is a term or collection of terms, followed by a subsidiary list (the **tail**), provided that the original list is not empty.

10.3.2   ATOMS AND CLAUSES

You saw how in Standard Syntax data was entered as a list: **(EEC BELGIUM 9.9 11.8)** was our first item of data, where four terms have been enclosed between the special pair of tokens (and). This fundamental form of data sentence is called an **atom**, and always has the form:

(relationship-name term1 term2 term3 . . .)

which is shown in manuals as

(R t1 t2 t3 . . . tk)

where R stands for the relationship-name and t1 t2 t3 for the next three terms, so there are k+1 terms in this general atom. The relationship-name is often referred to as the **predicate** of the atom, and micro-PROLOG is often referred to as using predicate logic.

This book has been based on the LPA (Logic Programming Associates) form of micro-PROLOG, which does use the (R t1 t2 t3 . . . tk) form of basic atom. There are other forms of PROLOG which use the basic atom in the form R(t1 t2 t3 . . . tk), namely the ESI (Expert Systems International) form. It is fairly easy to read programs in the other form when you are already acquainted with one form.

You will have noticed that in Standard Syntax an atom always began with a relationship name, the predicate which is a constant, never with a variable. In Logic Programming language the remaining terms in an atom are referred to as **arguments**. So, (R t1 t2 t3 . . . tk) is often described as:

(predicate argument1 argument2 argument3 . . . argumentk).

A **clause** is a collection of atoms or a list of sub-lists. If we look at the Standard Syntax rule:

&((HIGH-POP X)(EEC X Y Z)(LESS 20 Y))
&.

we can see this as a collection of atoms, and you will recall that I showed that there is the underlying implication:

(HIGH-POP X) if **(EEC X Y Z)** and **(LESS 20 Y)**

So we can say that the general form of a clause is

((atom)(atom1)(atom2)(atom3) . . . (atomk))

with the implication

((atom) if (atom1) and (atom2) and (atom3) . . . and (atomk))

Also the first sub-list (atom) in this case, is referred to as the **head** of the clause, and the remaining sublists (atom1), (atom2) and so on, as the **body**. Obviously then, rules always come in the form of clauses.

10.3.3   THE SUPERVISOR

You can think of the **Supervisor** as the program through which you, the user, interact with all of the micro-PROLOG software. It is through this program that you enter, run, and edit programs, and then save them to disk and load them later when they are wanted.

It also provides the primitive relations or command of Standard Syntax PROLOG, which we have already met in capital letters in the Simple dialect. All of those which we met earlier in the chapter: &(. . .) which acted as **add**, the query operator **&?(. . .)**, the commands **PP** and **R**, the arithmetic operators **SUM** and **TIMES**, comparators **LESS** and **EQ**, and so on belong to the Standard Syntax. In addition to the operators which I introduced earlier there are facilities for adding and deleting clauses in **ADDCL** and **DELCL**. You will also have realised that **LIST ALL**, **KILL**, **LOAD** and **SAVE** have pretty well identical effects to their lower-case counterparts which we met in SIMPLE. As you enter data sentences the Supervisor makes a dictionary of the names of the relationships which you use, and so **LIST DICT** will list these names for you.

As you have realised by now the most significant feature of the language is that it lets you define relationships for your own use. This facility is particularly important for defining error messages. The Supervisor will give you an error number if you offend the basic rules of the language, and then you have to look up what the number refers to in the manual provided. Using a special **?ERROR?** predicate you can add your own error messages to these numbers, which may be as full or as cryptic as you wish. These messages may be stored away on disk and loaded for future use as required, using the ERRTRAP module which I describe shortly. Some messages have been stored in the SIMPLE module, and so you do get a number and cryptic message if you are using that facility.

10.3.4   MODULES

You should now appreciate what is meant when it is said that the Supervisor provides a 'working environment' for the language, but, as you will also have realised, this environment has some fairly severe restrictions, and so the facilities are extended by the creation and use of **modules**. These are programs which have themselves been written in micro-PROLOG and can be loaded into the memory of the machine and used when needed. Micro-PROLOG can be extended almost indefinitely in this way.

I have referred to certain of the systems modules as the need has arisen. The list of all of the modules which are supplied to me by Acorn for micro-PROLOG on the BBC model B micro, is shown below. You should be able to identify the use of most of these already. Let's try and get them into perspective, by concentrating on those which we know about for a start.

DEFTRAP	**EDITOR**
ERRTRAP	**EXPTRAN**
EXREL	**LOGIC**
MICRO	**MITSI**
MODULES	**PROGRAM**
SIMPLE	**SPYTRAC**
TOLD	**TRACE**
simtrac	

In our brief look at Standard Syntax programming you saw that the logic function 'AND' was implied between adjacent atoms of a clause. The Supervisor also provides a logic function 'OR', so by asking the questions in a sometimes tortuous way most queries can be posed of a data-base; but as I said earlier the operators **NOT**, **FORALL**, **IF** and **ISALL** are contained in a module called logic-mod which is stored in the file LOGIC.

We have also seen the action of the trace-mod module from the TRACE file. This module exports — gives to the user — the relation name **??**, which may be used in the same way as the **?** command, but which, if issued, gives a step by step evaluation of each query. You can use the spytrace-mod from the SPYTRAC file in a similar way to trace-mod, except that the spytrace-mod lets you select particular parts of the evaluation process to look at, with the **spy-on**, **spy-off** and **spy** (relationship) commands. It is particularly useful for looking at the entry/exit behaviour, as programs and data are passed to and from disk files.

Standard Syntax micro-PROLOG does not allow you to edit your programs and data directly. The editor-mod program in the EDITOR file lets you go to an individual record and make amendments within it, and there are also several commands which let you change the structure of the data-base: e.g. insert, delete (kill), append a new record, move and copy records and so on. To effect these changes you have to load editor-mod into your work-space.

We have not experienced the facilities offered by the exrel-mod, exrel standing for external relation, mainly because the programs we have written have been very small. If the RAM of your machine is fairly restricted, and your program contains lots of single atom clauses, then there may be very little space left in your machine when the program is loaded and run. You can use exrel-mod to create special files on a disk, so that the data is stored on the disk but erased from the work-space. All that remains in the work-space is a new clause containing the name of the relationship; and when that relationship is used in a program the appropriate segment of the disk is accessed. So for practical purposes it seems to the user that the relationships are still in the work-space, when they are really on disk. Yes, the processing will be a little slower but the reading in of data from the disk is quite automatic requiring no additional effort on the part of the user. This process of disk memory posing as RAM-type memory is called a **virtual memory** technique.

The file SIMPLE contains four modules. Its purpose is to provide extensions to those facilities found in the Supervisor, and thereby create a much more user friendly working environment, particularly designed to suit beginners to the language, and that is why I have used the SIMPLE dialect of the language throughout the first nine chapters of the book. The sentence syntax of SIMPLE is more friendly for the beginner than the clausal syntax of Standard. This means that the job of one of the modules is to translate the SIMPLE sentence structure into clausal form, and this is done by the module query-mod. This module also contains definitions of the query command (**is** and **which** etc.), as well as the other pre-defined relations which occur in SIMPLE and not in Standard Syntax.

The module program-mod contains all of the program development commands, e.g. add, delete, insert, list and so on. When a program has been developed this module can be deleted from the work-space, to make more room in the memory at 'run' time. If the program needs more development then the module can be loaded back into the work-space from the PROGRAM file, where it is stored separately.

The third module is logic-mod which exports the three definitions **NOT**, **FORALL** and **ISALL** to become the lower-case versions of these operators which we have used in our earlier programs. The fourth module is errmess-mod which provides the cryptic error messages which occur when using SIMPLE, and which are marginally better than just the error numbers. Still, as I have said before, you can elaborate on these messages yourself if you wish. The SIMPLE version of the TRACE file is stored in simtrac.

The MICRO file is best seen as being very similar to SIMPLE except that the language retains the clausal form rather than the sentence form of SIMPLE. For a start then you will realise that the query-mod module is not required, because there is no translation from sentence to clausal form. There are three modules: logic-mod, errmess-mod and micro-mod. The latter provides the extensions to the Supervisor.

Both SIMPLE and MICRO forms of the language can use the contents of the two files EXPTRAN and TOLD. The job of the module exptran-mod is to translate expressions, usually arithmetic or mathematical expressions, back into micro-PROLOG form from the more traditional computing form which exptran-mod allows. After loading EXPTRAN you can form expressions using the more usual arithmetic operators $+ - * /$ and $=$. If one expression E1 = z, and if a second E2 = $(x*x - 7*x)$, then, because you are allowed to make the two expressions equal, if E1 = E2, this is equivalent to saying:

$z = (x*x - 7*x)$

So, if x has a value before the program reaches this expression, the net effect is to make the variable z assume the value calculated by the right-hand side of the equation.

Using only a little imagination you can see that mathematical expressions may be evaluated more easily than with the facilities hitherto available. If you wished to you could solve quadratic expressions in the following way:

&which(x:x between (0 8) and –10 = (x*x –7*x))

This finds the solutions to the quadratic equation:

$x*x - 7*x + 10 = 0$ in the range 0 to 8.

The TOLD file houses the told-mod module, and this is used so that the user can talk to the program. It makes the program interactive in a way which is very similar to how we have used the combination of **PP** and **R** operators throughout several chapters. An example taken straight from the Acorn manual will give you the gist of what is going on:

&which(percent z:(mark x outof y) is-told and z = (x/y*100))
mark X outof Y ? ans 20 40
percent 50
mark X outof Y ? ans 15 60
percent 25
mark X outof Y ? just 40 120
percent 3.3333333E1
No (more) answers
&.

You realise that you now have SIMPLE, TOLD and EXPTRAN all in the work-space of the machine together. **is-told** is the command which solicits data to be told by the user to the program. This module can be used to give data to the program, to add whole date sentences, and, at a more advanced level, to add new relationships to the data-base. It is a very powerful facility in more advanced micro-PROLOG programming.

The remaining files on the distribution disk can be described quite briefly. ERRTRAP is a module which makes available to the user more sophisticated error trapping methods than those given by errmess-mod, but is designed for use only by MICRO in standard clausal form not in SIMPLE sentence format. The most common form of error in micro-PROLOG generally is not having a definition for a relationship at the point of evaluation in a run, usually due to an oversight or most likely through misspelling. Such a simple mistake could stop the run of a fairly long program and waste the user a lot of time and effort. DEFTRAP traps definition errors like this, and gives the user the chance to correct the error without the program actually aborting. In this way you can think of DEFTRAP as an extension of ERRTRAP.

The MODULE file contains the facilities for you to write your own modules. It is obvious to you by now that writing modules to suit your own particular work and investigations is the key to progress in micro-PROLOG programming. Modules can be wrapped up as self-contained units of rules and data, and, if they are written correctly, relationship names used in one module can be used in another without fear of confusion. Modules can be written which call other modules, and so on. This means that the design, writing and encapsulation of modules needs great care and attention, and the facilities in MODULE aid in this process.

The last file on the disk is MITSI, which stands for 'Man In The Street Implementation' of micro-PROLOG, which gives an even more friendly version of some aspects of Simple programming. It was devised by Jonathon Briggs of LPA to give beginners the opportunity of using even more natural English like commands with the language.

10.4   Where next?

This has been an introductory text at a fairly elementary level. There is so much more still to be done with micro-PROLOG and so it is difficult to give clear pointers as to where the reader should go next, because there are so many directions in which he/she could go. Further, as I said in the Introduction to the chapter, after the reader has reached a certain level of competence, the direction taken will depend largely on what tasks he/she is interested in tackling.

One way of looking at where to go next is to survey the topics not covered in this book. When micro-PROLOG is implemented by LPA for a particular micro-computer system, then the software is modified slightly to allow the language to take full advantage of the facilities of that particular system. I have been using the Acornsoft version but have said very little about how it fits into the BBC micro system. The software does, however, allow you access to the sound, graphics, machine code and operating system facilities of the BBC micro. So if, for example, you are planning to write some simple educational programs in micro-PROLOG for that micro, then there is a great challenge awaiting you to get the best out of the graphics of the machine to make the programs visually attractive. This will be true of course for other micro systems. Professional micro-PROLOG on the RM Nimbus with MS Windows is a revelation.

There are several programming topics which appear in books on micro-PROLOG, which I have studiously avoided, e.g. parsing of English sentences, board games strategies (of the 'noughts and crosses' species), critical path analysis, expert systems shells and so on. I have avoided them partly because I did not aim the level of this book at solving that complexity of problem, but largely because these topics have been so well explored in other texts. There are five other books which I would recommend both to broaden and deepen your studies of PROLOG.

1   *micro-PROLOG: Programming in Logic*
Clark and McCabe
Prentice-Hall

This is a classic micro-PROLOG text which was probably supplied to you with the software and manuals when you bought the software. Not only is it the authority on the LPA micro-PROLOG version of the language, but it also has a section on applications which makes it invaluable as a reference work.

2 *Programming in PROLOG*
Clocksin and Mellish
Springer-Verlag

This is the second classic PROLOG text covering very similar ground to that of 1 above, but not in LPA micro-PROLOG. You should have no difficulty in following the arguments and examples in this Edinburgh ESI dialect of the language — and it will well repay the effort.

3 *Beginning micro-PROLOG*
Richard Ennals
Ellis Horwood and Heinemann Computers in Education

This is a must for those who plan to use the language in an educational environment.

4 *Start Problem Solving with PROLOG*
Tom Conlon
Addison-Wesley

This gives a clear and thorough treatment of elementary problem solving, with some interesting sample programs which are worked through in detail.

5 *Programming in micro-PROLOG*
Hugh de Saram
Ellis Horwood

The clearest summary of LPA Standard Syntax micro-PROLOG that I have encountered.

If you are involved in business or administration I am sure that you cannot fail to see some possible application of micro-PROLOG programming to your work. If you are involved in education then you must see that micro-PROLOG or some very similar language is vital to the development of more meaningful software in the future — for certainly educational software is somewhat in the doldrums at present.

I hope that this book has given you the flavour of what may be achieved with such a language, and a glimpse of what the future may have in store. Join your local computer club and see if they are using micro-PROLOG; if not, start up an interest group there yourself. The British Computer Society has a vibrant Expert Systems group, with a branch not too far from you — you only have to be interested to join such a group. Read all you can absorb about Knowledge Engineering, Expert Systems, and Artificial Intelligence, you will soon see the relevance of a micro-PROLOG type language, if you have not already. I hope you have enjoyed this book, and wish you luck in your micro-PROLOG programming in the future.

Answers to exercises

Chapter 1

1.1 The CITIES data-base is given in Chapter 2 page 16.

1.2 The ANIMALS data-base
&list all
birds animals-with legs
frogs animals-with legs
crocodiles animals-with legs
lizards animals-with legs
tigers animals-with legs
humans animals-with legs
horses animals-with legs
crocodiles animals-with scales
lizards animals-with scales
snakes animals-with scales
fish animals-with scales
tigers animals-with hair-fur
humans animals-with hair-fur
horses animals-with hair-fur
dolphins animals-with hair-fur
whales animals-with hair-fur
&.

1.3(a) **&is(Lyon city-in France)**
YES
&is(Oslo city-in Sweden)
NO
&is(Manchester city-in UK)
NO
&.

The answer to this last query does of course not mean that Manchester is not a city in the UK, but that it is not in the data-base.

1.3(b) **&is(Stockholm capital-city)**
YES
&is(Milan capital-city)
NO
&.

1.3(c)   &is(Sweden member-of EEC)
NO
&is(France member-of EEC)
YES
&.

1.3(d)   &which(x:x city-in Italy)
Milan
Rome
No (more) answers
&.

1.3(e)   &which(x:Oslo city-in x)
Norway
No (more) answers
&.

1.3(f)   &which(x:x member-of EEC)
France
UK
Italy
Netherlands
No (more) answers
&.

Once again I emphasise that you only get four countries named as EEC members in this query, because only these four have been entered into our data-base.

1.3(g)   &which(x:UK member-of x)
EEC
No (more) answers
&which(x:Norway member-of x)
No (more) answers
&.

1.4(a)   &is(dolphins animals-with hair-fur)
YES
&is(birds animals-with hair-fur)
NO
&.

1.4(b)   &which(x:crocodiles animals-with x)
legs
scales
No (more) answers
&which(x:horses animals-with x)
legs
hair-fur
No (more) answers
&.

1.4(c)   which(x:x animals-with hair-fur)
tigers
humans
horses
dolphins

whales
No (more) answers
&which(x:x animals-with legs)
birds
frogs
crocodiles
lizards
tigers
humans
horses
No (more) answers
&.

Chapter 2

2.1(a)   **&which(x:x animals-with hair-fur and x animals-with legs)**
tigers
humans
horses
No (more) answers
&.

2.1(b)   **&which(x:x animals-with hair-fur and**
1not x animals-with legs)
dolphins
whales
No (more) answers
&.

2.1(c)   **&which(x:x animals-with legs and**
1not x animals-with hair-fur and
1not x animals-with scales)
birds
frogs
No (more) answers
&.

2.1(d)   **&which(x:y animals-with x and**
1not y animals-with legs)
scales
scales
hair-fur
hair-fur
No (more) answers
&.

Note again how micro-PROLOG gives the characteristics for all of the animals in the data-base with the rather pedantic repetition for the cases of snakes, fish, dolphins and whales.

2.2   To save a little space in the book I have not included the **which** statements, but just the rules:

2.2(a) &list daughter-of
X daughter-of Y if
Y parent-of X and
X female
&which(x y:x daughter-of y)
Anne Philip
Anne Elizabeth
No (more) answers
&.

2.2(b) &list brother-of
X brother-of Y if
Z parent-of Y and
Z parent-of X and
X male
&which(x y:x brother-of y)
Charles Charles
Charles Anne
William William
Henry William
William Henry
Henry Henry
Charles Charles
. . .

The above data is repeated for the 'second' parent. To make the rule more precise you should really include a sentence to eliminate **Charles brother-of Charles** and similar solutions. This clause would have the form **and not X equal-to Y**, or using the **EQ** operator of Chapter 4, **and not X EQ Y**.

2.2(c) &list paternal-grandfather-of
X paternal-grandfather-of Y if
X father-of Z and
Z father-of Y
&which(x y:x paternal-grandfather-of y)
Philip William
Philip Henry
No (more) answers
&.

2.2(d) &list maternal-grandfather-of
X maternal-grandfather-of Y if
X father-of Z and
Z mother-of Y
&which(x y:x maternal-grandfather-of y)
No (more) answers
&.

2.3 I assume that the ANIMALS data-base is in the computer's memory.

2.3(a) &list animals-with-fur
X animals-with-fur if
X animals-with hair-fur

2.3(b)   &list animals-without-legs
          X animals-without-legs if
              X animals-with Y and
              not X animals-with legs

2.3(c)   &list animals-with-fur-without-legs
          X animals-with-fur-without-legs if
              X animals-with-fur and
              X animals-without-legs
          &which(x:x animals-with-fur-without-legs)
          dolphins
          whales
          No (more) answers
          &.

2.4   The MURDER data-base which I devised looks like:

          &list all
          A motive-is jealousy
          B motive-is financial-gain
          C motive-is grudge
          E motive-is financial-gain
          F motive-is grudge
          B access-to-weapon
          C access-to-weapon
          E access-to-weapon
          F access-to-weapon
          A opportunity-level high
          B opportunity-level medium
          C opportunity-level medium
          D opportunity-level high
          E opportunity-level low
          F opportunity-level high
          &.

2.4(a)   &which(x y:x motive-is y and x opportunity-level high)
          A jealousy
          F grudge
          No (more) answers
          &.

2.4(b)   &which(x y:x motive-is financial-gain and
          1x opportunity-level y)
          B medium
          E low
          No (more) answers
          &.

2.4(c)   &which(x:x access-to-weapon and x opportunity-level high)
          F
          No (more) answers
          &.

2.4(d)   &list strong-suspect
X strong-suspect if
      X opportunity-level medium
X strong-suspect if
      X opportunity-level high
&which(x:x strong-suspect)
B
C
A
D
F
No (more) answers
&.

2.4(e)   &list prime-suspect
X prime-suspect if
      X strong-suspect and
      X access-to-weapon
&which (x:x prime-suspect)
B
C
F
No (more) answers
&.

Chapter 4

4.1(a)   &which(x:SUM(382798.45 1987.32 x))
384785.77

To save a little space I will omit **No (more) answers** and the **&.** on the following
line from the answers in this chapter.

4.1(b)   &which(x:SUM(7234.25E6 36.8942E8 x))
1.092367E10

4.1(c)   &which(x:SUM(x 7194.65 9822.99))
2628.34

4.1(d)   &which(x:SUM(x 21.85E-4 9.742E-3))
7.557E-3

4.1(e)   &which(x:SUM(x 42.98 1.092367E10))
1.092367E10

4.1(f)   &which(x:TIMES(8462.37 9427.82 x))
79781701.1

4.1(g)   &which(x:TIMES(12.86E8 7.554E9 x))
9.714444E18

4.1(h)   &which(x:TIMES(x 2894.71 7944.37))
2.74444418

4.1(i)   &which(x:TIMES(x 21.79E7 79.43E-4))
3.64525011E-11

4.1(j)   &which(x:TIMES(x 56.82E-7 79.43E-4))
1397.92327

4.2(a)(i)   &which(x y:SUM(3742.62 976.83 x) and x INT y)
4719.45 4719

4.2(a)(ii)   &which(x y:TIMES(493.22 63.82 x) and x INT y)
31477.3004 31477

4.2(a)(iii)   &which(x y:TIMES(1.04E5 9.63E3 x) and x INT y)
1.00152E9 1.00152E9

4.2(a)(iv)   &which(x y:TIMES(x 5.843E8 7.983E12) and x INT y)
13662.5021 13662

4.2(b)(i)   &which(x y:SUM(35 –83 x) and TIMES(x 14 y))
–48 –672

4.2(b)(ii)   &which(x y:TIMES(35 1.8 x) and SUM(x 32 y))
63 95

4.2(c)   &is(TIMES(5 279 x) and TIMES(y 15 x) and y INT)
YES
&.

4.2(d)   &is(TIMES(x 749 68.42) and x LESS 0.1)
YES
&.

Chapter 5

5.1(a)   &list all
Elizabeth mother-of (Charles Anne)
Diana mother-of (William Henry)
Philip father-of (Charles Anne)
Charles father-of (William Henry)
(Elizabeth Anne Diana) female
(Philip Charles William Henry) male
&.

5.1(b)   (France UK Italy Netherlands) member-of EEC
(Paris London Rome Oslo Stockholm) capital-city
(Lyon Paris) city-in France
(Birmingham London) city-in UK
. . . and so on for **city-in** . . .

5.1(c)   (birds frogs crocodiles lizards tigers humans horses) animals-
with legs
(crocodiles lizards snakes fish) animals-with scales
(tigers humans horses dolphins whales) animals-with hair-fur

5.2   To include the data generated by the queries in this question would eat up valuable pages in the book, so for the first six questions I give only the **which** statements themselves.

5.2(a)   &which(x x1 x2 x3 x4 x5 x6:x description(x1 x2 x3 x4 x5 x6)
land x1 EQ f)

5.2(b)   The first line of the query will remain the same, so continue
l and 40 LESS x2)

5.2(c)   land x1 EQ f and 40 LESS x2)

5.2(d)   land x3 EQ t)

5.2(e)   land x1 EQ f and 40 LESS x2 and x3 EQ t)

5.2(f)(i)   land x5 EQ l and x6 EQ bl)

5.2(f)(ii)   land 40 LESS x2 and x3 EQ t and x4 EQ h)

5.2(g)   &list large
(X Y Z x y z X1) large if
X description (Y Z x y z X1) and
x EQ t and
y EQ h
&which(x:x large)

5.2(h)   &list dark
(X Y Z x y z X1) dark if
X description (Y Z x y z X1) and
z EQ d and
X1 EQ br
&which(x:x dark)

5.2(i)   &which(x:x large and x dark)

5.3   The first 10 records in the HOUSES data-base are:

WW14 REF-FOR (WW D 3 2 0 L 55000)
CI23 REF-FOR (CHI D 5 3 2 M 16800)
PW48 REF-FOR (PW D 3 1 1 M 69995)
OR09 REF-FOR (ORP T 3 1 0 S 28500)
BE73 REF-FOR (BEX D 4 2 1 M 52750)
BI37 REF-FOR (BIC F 1 1 0 N 22950)
PW19 REF-FOR (PW D 3 2 1 L 69950)
OR63 REF-FOR (ORP M 3 1 1 N 29950)
CI50 REF-FOR (CHI D 5 3 2 M 95000)
BR82 REF-FOR (BR S 4 3 0 S 36250)
. . . and so on.

The structure of the file is that shown in the question, with the abbreviations for
Area names: **WW** for West Wickham, **CHI** for Chislehurst, **PW** for Petts Wood,
OPR for Orpington, **BEX** for Bexley, **BI** for Bickley, and **BR** for Bromley.
To pick out those houses whose price is less £50000 you would enter the query

&which(x x1 x2 x3 x4 x5 x6 x7:x REF-FOR (x1 x2 x3 x4 x5 x6 x7)
land x7 LESS 50000)

and for those houses under £50000 with a large garden, you would repeat the first
line and continue

land x7 LESS 50000 and x6 EQ L)

To find detached houses with at least four bedrooms, you could change **at least 4** into **greater than 3**, and the second line of the query would become:

land x2 EQ D and 3 LESS x3)

To find a house in either Petts Wood or Orpington you could enter a second line like:

land (either x1 EQ OPR or x1 EQ PW)

Chapter 6

6.1(a)   &which(x:x item-in (a e i o u)
              land x item-in (r e c u r s i o n))
              e
              i
              o
              u
              No (more) answers
              &.

6.1(b)   &which(x:x item-in (8 13 11 14 9 6 10 12)
              land TIMES(y 2 x) and y INT)
              8
              14
              6
              10
              12
              No (more) answers
              &.

6.1(c)   &which(x:x item-in (2.37 –4.12 3.96 –2.21 –0.17 1.98)
              land x LESS 0)
              –4.12
              –2.21
              –0.17
              No (more) answers
              &.

6.1(d)   &which(x y:x item-in (3 7 5 11 9 14)
              land TIMES(x x y))
              3 9
              7 49
              5 25
              11 121
              9 81
              14 196
              No (more) answers
              &.

6.1(e)   &which(x y:x item-in (3 7 5 11 9 14)
              land SUM(y 3 x))
              3 0
              7 4

          5 2
          11 8
          9 6
          14 11
          No (more) answers
          &.

6.1(f)   &which(x y:x item-in (16 19 21 17 14)
          land TIMES(x 1.8 z) and SUM(z 32 y))
          16 60.8
          19 66.2
          21 69.8
          17 62.6
          14 57.2
          No (more) answers
          &.

Chapter 7

7.1   &list all
       1 sumnat 1
       X sumnat Y if
              1 LESS X and
              SUM(Z 1 X) and
              Z sumnat x and
              SUM(X x Y) and
              PP(X Y Z x)
       &which(x:9 sumnat x)
       2 3 1 1
       3 6 2 3
       4 10 3 6
       5 15 4 10
       6 21 5 15
       7 28 6 21
       8 36 7 28
       9 45 8 36
       45
       No (more) answers
       &.

7.2 Assuming that the ROYAL3 data-base is in the work-space of the machine, then you can add the **ancestor** rule:

&list ancestor-of
X ancestor-of Y if
       X parent-of Y
X ancestor-of Y if
       Z parent-of Y and
       X ancestor-of Z
&which(x y:x ancestor-of y)
Philip Charles
Philip Anne

Charles William
Charles Henry
Elizabeth Charles
Elizabeth Anne
Diana William
Diana Henry
Philip William
Elizabeth William
Philip Henry
Elizabeth Henry
No (more) answers
&.

7.3 If you take the **syns search** program given in the text and kill all of the **found-in** rules, you can use **item-in** to define a new version of **found-in** which can cope with synonym lists of variable length. I have also changed the **are-syns** data sentences to give an idea how you can use this program to act as a Translator program. I have not refined it in any way, but I am sure that you will readily see how the program could be improved. The same program could easily be modified to transpose melodies or chords in one musical key to another, so it is fairly useful program skeleton generally.

&list found-in
X found-in Y if
  are-syns Y and
  X item-in Y
&.
Remember 'item-in' must also be added to the data-base.
&list are-syns
are-syns (big grande gravido grosso importante)
are-syns (cold freddo raffreddato riservato)
are-syns (dark buio oscuro tenebroso)
are-syns (hard compatto difficile duro)
are-syns (heavy pesante opprimente violente)
are-syns (large grande abbondante ampio spazioso)
are-syns (pretty bellino carino grazioso)
are-syns (small piccolo minuscolo)
are-syns (smart bruciore dolore acuto)
are-syns (strict esatto severo stretto)
are-syns (tall alto grande esagerato incredible)
are-syns (uncouth goffo grottesco rozzo)
&search syns

What is your word ?small

Here is a list of synonyms
which includes your word

(small piccolo minuscolo)

What is your word ?goffo

Here is a list of synonyms
which includes your word

(**uncouth goffo grottesco rozzo**)

What is your word?

. . . and so on . . .

The text would have to be changed, but most changes would only have to be of a cosmetic nature to make this program quite useful.

Chapter 8

8.3   The squares of the values given in a list can be found by:

&which(x y:x item-in (1 2 3 4 5) and TIMES(x x y))
1 1
2 4
3 9
4 16
5 25
&.
No (more) answers
&.

Now put these squares into a list using **isall**:

&which(z:z isall(y:x item-in (1 2 3 4 5)
2and TIMES(x x y)))
(1 4 9 16 25)
No (more) answers
&.

So far you have needed only **item-in** in your work-space, but if you now wish to add up these values you will have to load in the **total-is** program:

&which(z x1:z isall(y:x item-in (1 2 3 4 5)
2and TIMES(x x y))
1z total-is x1)
(1 4 9 16 25) 55
No (more) answers
&.

8.5   **&list del**
     del (X Y Z) if
          (x (X|y)) append-to Y and
          (x y) append-to Z
     &.

8.8   My version of a bubble sort is shown below. The **bubble-sort** rule is recursive with an ending condition in the first rule that the list it has produced is ordered. This routine calls the **bubble** rule whose effect was described in the question, and is shown below. The ordered rule we used in the chapter and saw that it needed **link-in** and **lesseq** to do its work.
     To ring the changes, I have shown the program in the Micro-PROLOG Professional form from LPA, which precedes each variable with __, so **X, Y** and **Z**

become **__X**, **__Y** and **__Z**. This version allows you to use any word you like as a variable name, instead of just **X Y Z x y z** and so on as described in this book, provided you precede it with the **__**. So instead of **x** in one of the queries, I have used **__sorted-list** as a variable word. I will leave you to judge how much of an advantage you think this may be, after you have written a few programs.

```
&list all
__X bubble-sort __X if
        __X ordered
__X bubble-sort __Y if
        __X bubble __Z and
        __Z bubble-sort __Y
(__X) bubble (__X)
(__X __Y | __Z) bubble (__X | __x) if
        __X LESS __Y and
        (__Y | __Z) bubble __x
(__X __Y | __Z) bubble (__Y | __x) if
        not __X LESS __Y and
        (__X | __Z) bubble __x
__X ordered if
        (forall (__Y __Z) link-in __X
        then __Y lesseq __Z)
(__X __Y) link-in (__X __Y) | __Z)
(__X __Y) link-in (__Z | __x) if
        (__X __Y) link-in __x
__X lesseq __X
__X lesseq __Y if
        __X LESS __Y
&.
```

Before trying out the whole **bubble-sort** program, let's try out **bubble** on its own. It only deals with one bubble at a time, but by running it several times, each time writing as a query the results of the previous query you can see how it will work.

```
&which(x:(5 4 3 2 1) bubble x)
(4 3 2 1 5)
No (more) answers
&which(x:(4 3 2 1 5) bubble x)
(3 2 1 4 5)
No (more) answers
&which(x:(3 2 1 4 5) bubble x)
(2 1 3 4 5)
No (more) answers
&which(x:(2 1 3 4 5) bubble x)
(1 2 3 4 5)
No (more) answers
&.
```

As I said in the question, the program does not know that there is only one sorted sequence to be found, so even after it has one it will proceed to search for others. You can anticipate this by using a **one**-query rather than a **which**-query, but as you can see from the **which**-query, you can stop the processing after one solution by the **and** /, which can be read as 'and then stop'. So, this query reads 'find the first sorted list and then stop'.

&one(x:(7 6 5 4 3 2 1) bubble-sort x)
(1 2 3 4 5 6 7)
more?(y/n)n
&which(x:(9 1 8 2 7 3 6 4 5) bubble-sort x and /)
(1 2 3 4 5 6 7 8 9)
No (more) answers
&.

The next query shows the use of **__sorted-list** as a variable rather than **x**, and the last shows that the program will handle lists of characters just as well as numbers.

&which(__sorted-list:(7 6 5 4 3 2 1) bubble-sort __sorted-list and /)
(1 2 3 4 5 6 7)
No (more) answers
&.

&which(x:(u h b t f c e s a) bubble-sort x and /)
(a b c e f h s t u)
No (more) answers
&.

Index